WEALTH

FOR ALL

AFRICANS

WEALTH

FOR ALL

AFRICANS

How Every African Can Live the Life of Their Dreams

IDOWU KOYENIKAN

GRANDEUR TOUCH, LLC

Copyright © 2014 by Idowu Koyenikan

All rights reserved. No part of this publication may be reproduced, distributed, or transmitted in any form or by any means, including photocopying, recording, or other electronic or mechanical methods, without the prior written permission of the publisher, except in the case of brief quotations embodied in critical reviews and certain other noncommercial uses permitted by copyright law. For permission requests, write to the publisher, addressed "Attention: Permissions Coordinator," at the address below.

Grandeur Touch, LLC
1421 E. Broad Street
Suite 329
Fuquay-Varina, NC 27526
U.S.A

Ordering Information:
Quantity sales. Special discounts are available on quantity purchases by corporations, associations, and others. For details, contact the publisher at the address above or visit www.ikelevates.com.

Printed in the United States of America

First Edition

ISBN 978-0-9906397-0-1

DEDICATION

I dedicate this book to God, through whom all things are possible, to my wife, Ashley, and to my son, Samuel.

CONTENTS

Preface	vi
Introduction: Lessons from the Serengeti	viii
Lesson I: Wisdom	1
Chapter 1: The Wisdom of Money	5
Chapter 2: Mediocrity	11
Chapter 3: One-Minute Millionaire	16
Chapter 4: Education	22
Chapter 5: Personal Development	27
Lesson II: Empowerment	32
Chapter 6: Poverty	36
Chapter 7: Entrepreneurship	42
Chapter 8: Mindset	48
Chapter 9: Women and the Youth	54
Chapter 10: Daily Affirmations	61
Lesson III: Action	66
Chapter 11: Fear and Other Obstacles to Success	70
Chapter 12: How Strong Is Your "Why"?	77
Chapter 13: The Power of Focus	82
Chapter 14: Planning and Goal Setting	87
Chapter 15: Focus on the Process and Not the Result	93
Lesson IV: Leadership	99
Chapter 16: Personality and Character	104
Chapter 17: Developing Relationships	110
Chapter 18: Resilience	115
Chapter 19: Time Management	121
Chapter 20: What Would "They" Think? What Would "They" Say?	127
Lesson V: Trust	132
Chapter 21: Branding	135
Chapter 22: It Takes a Village	141
Chapter 23: Trust and Believe That You Have What It Takes	146
Chapter 24: Trust the Process	151
Lesson VI: Honor	158
Chapter 25: Honor Your Purpose	161
Chapter 26: Giving Back	166
Chapter 27: Leaving a Legacy	171
Chapter 28: The African Pride	177

PREFACE

I was born in Lagos, Nigeria, where I spent my formative years. I am writing this book today as my way of giving back to Africa, the continent, the culture, and the land where my journey through life began. I am also writing this book because of the vision that I have of a better Africa, where its people and the continent as a whole live up to their potential. I want to let every African know that regardless of their beginnings, background, or current situation, that achieving greatness is possible; it is possible for them to live out their dreams.

My hope is that this book will inspire change in your life and you will in turn inspire change in your community. I believe there is no greater gift than wisdom. A gift of money might change your situation for a day, a week, or even a year, but the application of wisdom will change your life forever. Through this book, my hope is that the wisdom and principles that you will learn will change your life and Africa forever.

Wealth as discussed in this book does not only refer to money or material wealth, as most people think. I consider wealth to mean freedom, good health, happiness, good relationships, success, financial independence, and all the other dreams, goals, and objectives that you might have. There are a lot of books out there on this subject, but most of them talk about strategies that are not available to the average African. Most of those books were not even written with Africans in mind. My goal is to change that. This book is geared toward the strategies, techniques, tools, and resources that are available to all Africans. The simplistic nature of the book is intended with no overly complicated strategies introduced. The intention is to have it be easy enough for people of various age groups to easily digest the content. The book touches on the mindset, cultural backgrounds, and outlook of Africans that most books do not address.

The acronym for WEALTH as used in this book stands for Wisdom, Empowerment, Action, Leadership, Trust, and Honor, which are all necessary tools to achieve success and a wealthy life. I will be touching on the positives and negatives of African culture and how it all affects your shot at success.

Preface

This book will enlighten you by addressing the various issues of importance to Africans. I have found out that in order for the average African to obtain wealth, a lot of changes and sacrifices must be made, ranging from how you *think* to the way you *do* things. This book will present a lot of practical ideas and things to do; if you follow them carefully, they *will* lead to wealth. It is your duty to identify and implement the idea that best fits your situation.

INTRODUCTION: LESSONS FROM THE SERENGETI

One of the greatest animal spectacles in the world is the annual Serengeti migration. The annual migration is of wildebeests, zebras and gazelles in Eastern Africa, covering areas around Kenya and Tanzania. For nature lovers and animal enthusiasts, to witness this firsthand would be worth your while and an experience you will never forget.

During the migration, these animals face a difficult dilemma where, if they do not move, they will die. Throughout the year, they make a journey in a complete loop, searching for food and water. Along the way, they encounter predators such as crocodiles, lions, leopards, and hyenas that prey on the weak and feeble among the herd. Most of these predators eagerly await the migration and have timed their feeding cycle to coincide with it. They gather in large numbers along the path of the migrating herd, hoping to make a kill, knowing this is their big chance.

The herds of animals are made up of newborn, young, and adult animals. Young wildebeests are unlike other animals in that just a few minutes after birth, a newborn can start running along with the rest of the herd. It must do this quickly or risk death. Their ability to become mobile quickly increases their chances of survival, but it does not guarantee that they will make the entire journey alive.

One part of their journey that attracts a lot of interest from tourists is the crossing of the Grumeti and Mara rivers. These rivers have massive crocodiles, which patiently wait to feast on the animals as they try to cross the river. The crocodiles have memorized the path where the animals cross; they lie, perfectly positioned, waiting for the herd.

The older and more experienced animals of the herd are better at crossing the river than the younger ones, of course. The crocodiles also, from experience, are aware that the younger animals are the easier target, as they are physically weaker than the older animals, giving the crocodiles an added advantage.

The crocodiles attack the animals in a feeding frenzy, and when it is all over, only some of the herd make it across the river to the other side. These animals will continue on their

Introduction: Lessons from the Serengeti

journey while the crocodiles feast on the animals that were not so successful.

The animals that made it will be safe from the crocodiles for now, until the next time they cross paths at the river again. While they might have safely escaped that situation, several other predators must be faced along the way as the herd continues its journey. These predators, like the lion, eagerly await the herd; they are primed and ready to feast on them.

Just like the wildebeests, zebras, and gazelles, humans are also on a journey through life, throughout which we search for food and water, success, happiness, and, among other things, we search for love. Just like these animals face different hardships and predators along their journey, there are also many obstacles in our way that try to stop us from getting the things we want, some of which are crucial for our existence. If we do not overcome these obstacles, we do not get what we want.

The annual migration is not just about animals moving from place to place; it is really a journey about survival. It is also a journey of learning, pursuing goals, growth, and the hope of success. The animals' journey teaches us many life lessons that will be addressed in this book. The first letter of each one of the lessons serves as an acronym and spells out the word WEALTH:

WISDOM
EMPOWERMENT
ACTION
LEADERSHIP
TRUST
HONOR

There is a particularly tense moment when the animals arrive at the edge of the Grumeti and Mara rivers. Standing at the edge, their hearts pounding with fear, they look into the river and see hungry crocodiles waiting to tear them apart. The crocodiles stare right back at the herd, waiting for the animals to make a move. You can almost hear the heartbeats of the herd. Now imagine the thoughts of those animals. They can see

Introduction: Lessons from the Serengeti

their destination across the river and they can also see that the only way for them to get there is through this river, which is infested with crocodiles snapping their jaws filled with razor-sharp teeth.

The older animals are more experienced, wiser, and physically and mentally stronger than the other animals. They have successfully crossed the river many times before; they know what to expect from the crocodiles and what they need to do to cross. The younger animals, on the other hand, are not so experienced. For this very reason, the crocodiles target the younger animals because they know that they are not as wise as the older animals. **WISDOM** as evidenced here is a very important attribute for success. It increases your chances of succeeding at whatever you do in the same way that it does for the wiser animals.

Humans face difficult situations, just like these animals at the edge of the rivers. We feel the need to "cross over" to reach our goals, dreams, and ambitions, but various obstacles prevent us from getting there. We look at our goals and ambitions, and, just like the animals, we fear the crocodiles; the obstacles that we face frighten us. We say to ourselves, "I am not going to make it through this situation. It is impossible for me to do it." We convince ourselves that there is no way we can achieve our goals, dreams, ambitions, or whatever we want in life. As we focus on these negative thoughts, they terrify us even further, when instead we should focus on thoughts that empower us, thoughts that unlock the power within us and help us overcome the obstacles we face, thoughts such as, "This is possible," and not thoughts of "This is impossible."

Another way to empower ourselves and overcome our obstacles is to ask the right kind of questions, such as, "How do I make it through this situation? What do I need to do to get across?" When you ask yourself questions like these, your mind immediately starts to look for solutions to solve your problem instead of just focusing on the problem alone. In times like these, you also need to draw from your inner strength and firmly believe that nothing is impossible. You must say to yourself, "I will get through this and I will get to the other side where my goals and dreams await me." Your will to get through to the other side has to be stronger than the will of the crocodile, or whatever obstacle that lies ahead of you. By doing this, you will feel empowered and ready to take on the challenge. The feeling of **EMPOWERMENT** is therefore a very important element for your success. Empowering yourself at the right moment will also give you the drive you need to succeed.

When we face obstacles in our lives, it's easy to quit and not to even try. Fear can cause you to be stagnant and prevent you from attempting to even reach your goal. Some people wait around for miracles, hoping that what they want will magically happen without them having to take any action on their part. I think again of the herd of animals when they get to the edge of the river and they are staring right at the crocodiles. Most animals make it across the river partly because they took action. If they simply stood at the edge of the river and never made any attempt to cross at all, then they would simply remain at the edge of the river. What if, while they are at the edge of the river, some animals decide to wait for something magical to transport them across without any effort on their part? Will it happen? No. They would not achieve their goal until they make an attempt. As humans, we also need to know that if we do not take action toward our goals, we cannot expect them to magically happen. **ACTION** is therefore an important element of achieving the success we desire.

The herd mentality dictates that the rest of the animals follow a leader on their journey. The animal in front must lead the rest of the herd in the right direction, or else all the animals will end up in the wrong place. Leadership is therefore a crucial quality; a leader's decision affects the lives of many, and not just its own. The success rate of the herd of animals crossing the river increases if the leader finds a path through the river with no crocodiles. By doing this, the leader gives the animals a greater chance to survive. In the same way, a good leader in the workplace, government, school, or wherever can also show his people or followers the right path to success and prosperity. A good leader should always strive to do this. Good **LEADERSHIP** is therefore a vital attribute, not just for your personal success, but also for the success of others.

Introduction: Lessons from the Serengeti

On the journey, the animals must trust their instincts, their interpretation of the environment, and other factors they encounter along the way. They must trust their decision-making process in when to stop or move in their search for food and water. They must trust that the direction that they are going is the right one and trust that they will reach their destination. They also must trust their instincts when they sense danger and to act appropriately so that they can avoid predators along the way. When one animal senses danger and takes off in a certain direction, the rest of the animals also run away, even when they are not aware of what the danger is. They do this because they trust and believe in the herd. Humans also must trust themselves and their abilities. We have to know deep inside that nothing is impossible; whatever we set our minds to, we can accomplish.

Just like the animals, sometimes you also must trust your instincts and your intuition. The animals rely on this to find food and to keep them out of danger. You have to trust it even when it asks you to go where nobody else would go, to do something nobody else would do. You just have to trust it; when you do, you will be rewarded. **TRUST** as demonstrated here is therefore a key element to our success.

When the animals make it across the river, I have no doubt that they feel honored to have beaten the odds and attained their goal. Imagine what goes through their minds after crossing the river, knowing that others did not make it. Imagine what they think when they look back to where they started and at all the crocodiles in the river they managed to escape. We feel the same way when we overcome any obstacle in our life. When you attain the goals that you set for yourself against all odds, it makes you feel good inside. A great sense of honor comes over you to have had such success. **HONOR** is one of the highest levels of prestige you can ever attain.

One of the important things at play here in the story about the animals and their migration is the power of choice: The animals have a choice to move or not to move, to cross or not to cross the river, to follow or not to follow the herd. They have a choice to search for food and water, or remain behind and die. The different choices that the animals make ultimately affect their chances of survival. Unlike these animals, we are

Introduction: Lessons from the Serengeti

not limited in the choices we can make; we have a full array available to us, in fact. Our options and possibilities in life are endless. We also have the ability to follow through with the choices that we make.

Success results from choices you make every day. When you make a choice, your mind sends out a message to the part of your body that is responsible for carrying out that choice to do so. Sometimes other people make choices for you with or without your knowledge. There are, however, certain choices in life that other people cannot make for you. These are choices that you have to make for yourself. The choice to do whatever it takes to overcome an obstacle that you face is an example of a choice that must come from within. If someone else makes the choice for you, you may easily back down when things get tough.

In life, obstacles of all shapes and sizes will obscure your goal, but you have to keep moving, irrespective of what you face. Just like the crocodiles know exactly where and when the animals would try to cross the river, it almost seems like the obstacles know where and when to get in your way. The obstacles often appear when you feel low, during times when you are vulnerable, defeated, and when it is easy for you to quit. To combat this, you must know what to expect when these obstacles appear, a topic we will go into further in this book.

These obstacles also help you grow and become stronger. The young animals that get through the crocodiles are better prepared the next time they meet them again. Similarly, every obstacle you encounter makes you better prepared for the future. When you come across the obstacle again, you know what to expect and how to achieve the success you want. Also, every obstacle you come across has a lesson to teach you; those lessons help you become a better person.

Sometimes, we must face these obstacles or our enemies on their ground, a place where they appear stronger (and where we are not as comfortable). The crocodiles have the advantage when they attack from the river because they are equipped with a tail and legs that are biologically adapted to move freely in the water. Some obstacles that we face also seem to attack from a position of significant advantage, but

Introduction: Lessons from the Serengeti

triumphing over these obstacles comes down to preparation. When you are well prepared, nothing can stop you. Your turf or not, success will be yours.

Irrespective of what rivers you try to cross in your life or what awaits you in that river, you can make it through. With the right preparation, you will get to the other side, where wealth, success, happiness, or everything you strive for awaits you. Always remember: **The moment you quit and stop fighting for what you want, what you don't want will take its place**. In this book, we will cover practical tools you can use to get the success you want. Read on and be encouraged as we go on this journey together. As you read on, firmly believe that your dreams are achievable. Nothing is impossible for you. Now, let the journey begin.

LESSON I: WISDOM

Over the years, I have worked with some of the wealthiest people in the world on various financial issues. I have worked on everything from helping them build on their wealth to protecting their wealth to distributing their wealth. I have studied their ways to see what sets them apart and how they can be so successful. Based on my experience working with them and the research that I have done, I found certain common principles among them. These principles are universally applicable, regardless of who you are or where you are in the world. Whatever your definition of success is, whether it's obtaining wealth, living a happy and fulfilled life, or having better relationships, these principles will help you achieve your success.

Most people have great ideas and "secrets" on how to get wealthy, but they keep it to themselves, fearing that if they tell too many people, they will lose their opportunity for wealth. I do not believe in this; I believe that when I help you live the life of your dreams and become better as a person, we all benefit from it. For that reason, I will not hold back the wisdom that I have acquired. Read on, and as you do, my hope is that this book will help you achieve the success you desire.

Wisdom is the key to all wealth and the basis for greatness. If you seek wisdom first and obtain it, everything else that you seek you will find. Wisdom shows you how to be successful by guiding you toward goals to shoot for and how to achieve those goals. Wisdom also shows you how to maintain your success when you become successful. The same thing applies to money. Wisdom shows you how to keep money when you make it, because making money is not enough if you end up losing it all. What good is it to have once had money when you have nothing to show for it? If you do not guard what you have wisely, you will lose it. Wisdom also shows you how to spend your money so it goes to the right places where it will do the most good. If you keep spending money unwisely, it will go out faster than it comes in, and when that happens, you will be out of money in no time. For these reasons, acquiring wisdom is critical for your success; in fact, wisdom and success go hand in hand.

Acquiring wisdom is great, but if you stop there, you will not get the results you want. **It is therefore important for you to remember that it is not only about acquiring wisdom, but, more importantly, it is about applying wisdom, which gets you the results you want.** The same goes for knowledge, ideas, information, and all other forms of wisdom. Putting wisdom to use should be your main goal, not just acquiring it.

I once had a great business idea that would have made me millions. For three years, I sat on that idea, doing nothing with it. One day, while reading the news, I found out that another company had implemented the same idea that I had and made lots of money with it. I felt terrible about myself. What I found out that day taught me a valuable lesson: **Wisdom and ideas do not make you money; execution and application do**.

Books are an excellent source of wisdom; they offer great knowledge and valuable insights about life. There are books written on just about every subject imaginable. You can become an expert in any chosen field if you are prepared to read the required materials. Biographies or autobiographies are also a good source of wisdom. They describe a person's life experiences, successes, failures, and lots of other great lessons that you can learn from. Through these books, you can learn from others' mistakes without having to make the same mistakes yourself. You can also learn how they were able to obtain their success in a short amount of time. For example, you could learn what it took someone else fifty years to learn in just a matter of minutes by reading a few pages. It is therefore an efficient way to use your time and to gain wisdom without adding extra years to your life. This is what makes it possible for a twenty-year-old to have the wisdom of a fifty-year-old person without necessarily being the age of fifty.

Wisdom is also about information. **Sometimes the difference between where you are and where you want to be is the information you have.** Information is important, and just like a key, it can unlock doors to opportunities and the success you seek. For example, the information you have could be the difference between getting a job and not getting a job. If you do not know that a particular company is hiring, how would you know to apply for a job there? If you do not apply for a particular job, how can you expect to get the job? Having the right information therefore matters; everything that you do is affected by the information you have.

Wisdom could also be the difference between life and death. Imagine someone who has no knowledge of how a tap works and is left in a house, all alone, for an extended period of time. Even though the house has running water that can be easily accessed through a tap, that person could die of thirst due to a lack of knowledge on how to operate a tap. If only the person knew how to turn on the tap, he or she could access all the water that is needed. The failure to do so would, however, lead to death from thirst. In the same way, there are many people out there that are dying. They could be dying financially, emotionally, spiritually, or even physically. Yet, the very wisdom that they need to survive is available to them. If only they would "turn on the tap" and access that wisdom. Don't let that be you. Seek the wisdom you need.

Every life experience that you have had has something to contribute to your life. There is no such thing as a wasted experience. This includes bad and unpleasant experiences. They, too, also have very important lessons to teach you, mainly how to avoid those bad and unpleasant situations in the future. Learn from your past mistakes; they have lessons to teach you, too. You can learn what you are doing wrong and how to better manage yourself if you ever find yourself in the same situation again.

Another source of obtaining wisdom is through advice. There are two kinds of advice: good and bad. Stay away from bad advice. Carefully analyze the advice you get from others before acting on it. People of every age from every walk of life always seem to have advice to give. Advice has to be one of the cheapest things there is because everyone gives it away freely. Be very careful who you take advice from. Do not be rude about it; listen to what the person has to say and then decide whether or not to follow the advice. If it sounds like something that does not make sense, you need to ignore it, research it some more, or discard it and continue your life. If it makes sense, find a way to incorporate it into your life. But don't follow anyone's advice blindly, regardless of who he or she is or where the advice is coming from.

Think about the motive behind the advice that you get. Ask yourself, "Why is this person giving me this advice? Is it because he or she cares about me, or is he or she just trying to lead me in the wrong direction?" Think about these things and then proceed with caution. Make sure you think thoroughly through these questions. Also, consider how credible the source of the advice is. Ask yourself, "Does this person really know what he or she is talking about? How did they come about the information they are passing on?" Do not underestimate anyone, but do not do what everyone tells you to do, either.

When you do not have wisdom, it will cost you a lot in time and resources. You will end up spending more time and money on something that could have cost you substantially less to achieve had you had wisdom. For that very reason, it is important to obtain it. Keep in mind that when you actively seek wisdom, it increases the degree to which you are able to find it. Be deliberate about seeking wisdom. Read books, be curious about things, learn by doing, and learn from others. Study people who are already great at what you are trying to do. Find out what they did differently. Find out what they know that you do not know. The information you find is wisdom that can change your life. Most importantly, when you obtain wisdom, do not forget to put it to use. **A genius in the wrong position could look like a fool.** You not only have to have wisdom and apply it, but you must also apply it in the right way and in the right place for it to make the biggest difference.

CHAPTER 1: THE WISDOM OF MONEY

Money is a great servant but a bad master.
—Francis Bacon

When you love and worship money, you become a servant to it; money becomes your master. Money can control you, making you do all sorts of things beyond what you would normally do. There is no limit to how far money can push you, which is why you must be very careful in your relationship to money. Money as a master can cause you to commit crime, do evil, and break your own rules in order to obtain it. Money can also encourage you to worship it, but to achieve your success, keep money in its place, where it belongs. Do not worship it.

When money becomes your servant, on the other hand, you are in control; you get to tell it what to do for you. If you are the master in this relationship, you can use money to fulfill your needs and wishes. If there is something you want to buy, you can go out and buy it. In the same way, if there is someone you want to help financially, you can help that person. As a master over money, you also have the authority to send out money to go out and make you more money. Just like a good servant, money can be obedient to you. **Money will do as you tell it to do, attracting more money and bringing it to its master if you show it how.**

Any master who treats his servants well often gets the same kind of treatment back from his servants. If you are a good steward of your money, you will reap the rewards of it. When money realizes that it is in good hands, it wants to stay and multiply in those hands. Treat money well and it would treat you well. Treat it badly, and it will leave you for someone else who will treat it well.

Money and People

Have you ever heard a comment similar to this before?: "Back in the day, John used to be a certain way, but as soon as he made money, he changed." I have heard comments like this many times, and I am sure you have, too. But while this is possible for some people, I do not believe money changes majority of people. **I believe having money only reveals more of who you already are.**

Money is neither good nor bad; money is neutral. It is all about what you use it for. If you like to help people, having more money allows you to do that. If you are the type of person that likes to party a lot, having more money allows you to party more. The reason why people think money changes people is that they never knew what was in that person's core in the first place. The person was just not able to express who he or she was due to financial conditions.

First, you work for money, and then money works for you. The majority of people start their careers working for others. The typical arrangement is to work for a company or an individual and get paid for the services you render. This is a good arrangement, provided you are getting paid fairly and justly. It is also typical for people that earn a living this way to adjust their everyday living based on what they earn. The ultimate lesson here, though, is that as you do this, you should always keep the long-term goal in mind, which is to first work for money and then let money work for you. You accomplish this by setting aside some of the money you earn and putting into a business or some other form of investment to benefit you later. **Money is always eager and ready to work for anyone who is ready to employ it.** Once you find the right opportunity, put money to work for you. This will increase your chances of reaching your financial goals.

The more your money works for you, the less you have to work for money. As money begins to work for you, you can slowly transition away from working for someone else for money. After a while, you will be able to manage your money as your full-time job through your business or investment. There will come a time in your life that you will no longer be able to work for money: retirement. Your physical strength diminishes as you get older, and when you cannot work any longer, you will need money working for you. Make arrangements for the day you retire, when you are no longer able to support your family through regular work.

Parkinson's Law

Often referred to as "Parkinson's Second Law," and named after Cyril Northcote Parkinson, this law states, "expenditures rise to meet income." To put this in simple terms, no matter how much you make, your expenses always have a way of catching up with your income. People tend to increase their expenses in direct proportion to their increased income. When this happens, the increase in expenses wipes away the increased income; overall, no extra money is created. This is a trap that many people fall for, something I see happen over and over again.

To beat this trap, the trick is to live below your means. When you increase your income, you do not have to go out and spend more money. If, for example, you are used to living in a certain house and paying a certain amount of rent, earning a higher income does not mean that you immediately have to move to a different house with a higher rent just because you now earn more money. Doing this only wipes away the additional money you now make. Be wary of Parkinson's Law and make sure you properly evaluate your decisions concerning increased income.

The Power of Interest Rates

Compound interest is often referred to as the eighth wonder of the world due to its magical powers. It involves earning interest on an original amount of money you have put away and then continuing to earn interest on the interest. It is even more magical if you can make new additions to what you have put away as it compounds. With this, your money continues to grow at a remarkable rate. Time is a primary component of the magic of compound interest. The longer you let your money compound, the greater it grows, so it is important to start early. It is also important to know that you do not have to start with a lot of money. Whatever amount of money you can put away will do, provided that you are consistent with putting money away and allowing it to compound. By doing this, your money will earn money and the earnings will earn more money.

Become familiar with the "rule of 72," which calculates how many years it takes for your money to double at a given interest rate. Divide 72 by the given interest rate; whatever result you get represents how many years it will take for your money to double at the given interest rate. If you currently earn a 10% rate of return on your money and you would like to know how long it takes to double it at this interest rate, divide 72 by 10. The resulting answer is 7.2, which means that your money would double every 7.2 years at a 10% rate of return. In the same way, if you currently earn a 12% rate of return, dividing 72 by 12 gives you 6, which means your money will double every 6 years at a 12% rate of return.

Organizing Your Finances Takes Discipline

Most people shy away from properly tracking their money, believing that accounting is tedious, unnecessary, boring, and that their time could be better spent doing something else. Even though you may not enjoy organizing your finances, you must learn to do it regularly. If you do not, you will find yourself always wondering where your money went. Whether it is with your personal finances or your business finances, you absolutely must take accounting seriously. It helps you develop better financial habits and shows you areas to focus on to improve your overall financial picture.

Organizing your finances, finding ways to improve it, and developing good saving habits require a lot of discipline on your part. But financial discipline should not be thought of as something that takes away your freedom or joy out of your life; it should instead be used as something that helps you get what you want out of life. Get your finances organized today and you will reap the rewards right away.

Increase Your Income or Decrease Your Expenses

Increasing your income and decreasing your expenses are two primary ways to grow your wealth. As simple as it sounds, people still struggle with it. Increasing your income involves finding ways to earn more money than you are currently earning. This can be done in a variety ways, such as finding a better-paying job, creating a different income stream other than your primary job, or exploring a number of the different opportunities addressed in this book. Decreasing your expenses is all about finding ways to cut down your spending, whether it's in the area of transportation, clothing, entertainment, housing, lifestyle choices, or elsewhere.

These choices necessitate that you constantly evaluate your needs versus your wants. Your needs are those absolute essentials, such as food and water. Your wants are not necessarily things that you have to have, but you desire to have them anyway, an example being having one pair of jeans in ten different colors. If there is something you absolutely do not have to have, then that would be a good place to start to decrease your expenses. You must find ways to eliminate or reduce those wants. Once that happens, don't regret the things you wanted but did not get. Successfully increasing your income or decreasing your expenses will free up more money for you; you can free up even more money when you do both.

The money you make is a symbol of the value you create. The value you demonstrate in the marketplace and to the world determines how much money you make. As an example, the president of a company earns more money than a security guard in the same company because the president is considered more valuable to the company. It is not because the president is a better person than the security guard, but in the monetary sense, the president helps the company make more money than the security guard does. For this reason, the company considers the president more valuable and so he is paid more.

The more value you can create, the more money you can make. If you have a job and you feel you deserve to make more than you do, make yourself more valuable to the company by taking on additional responsibilities or learning new skills and roles within the company.

You can make as much money as you believe you are worth, provided you take the steps necessary to make it a reality. Most people believe that they should make a certain amount of money, even though they are not currently doing so. They do nothing about it and expect it to magically happen. If you value yourself a certain way and you are not currently getting paid according to that value, what you need to do is to find what people who are getting paid that way are doing. What expertise do they have? What skills do they demonstrate? Once you find these things out, you must develop a plan of action for yourself to deliver a similar value.

CHAPTER 2: MEDIOCRITY

Definition of mediocre:
1. **of only ordinary or moderate quality; neither good nor bad; barely adequate**
2. **not satisfactory; poor; inferior**

—Dictionary.com

Growing up in Lagos, Nigeria, I had a tendency to settle for mediocrity. I am not quite sure where I picked up this habit, but it followed me around for a while. Worse still, I did not even know I had a problem with mediocrity until later on in my life. I was fine with things just being "okay" in my life. Mediocrity, as it so often does, started with one area of my life and spread into other areas from there. I did not push myself to reach the next level, a particularly apparent trait in my schoolwork. I did really well in school in my primary school days, but then things started to drop midway through my secondary school years.

With certain schoolwork, my thought process was to do just enough to pass. I would say to myself that I didn't have to get an "A" when all I needed was a passing grade to get promoted to the next class, and that is exactly what I did. I was stuck in this "passing" mindset until I got to the United States of America for my university education. It was there I learned about the concept of the grade point average (GPA). With this system, it was not just about passing the class anymore; it showed how well I passed the class.

I tried to get the highest grade possible in every class, as those grades would follow me throughout my university education. If I started out with low grades, it would require a lot more effort on my part to try to increase my GPA by scoring higher grades in the other classes. Depending on how low the grades were, I might even have to retake the entire class again just so I could replace the low grade with a higher grade. **When you start things out in a mediocre way, you have to work a lot harder to make up for being mediocre.**

My mother used to tell me that anything that is worth doing is worth doing well. Back then, it did not mean much to me. But as I went through different life experiences, it all began to make sense. We are not meant to go through life just being "okay." We are meant to be the best that we can be. Everything that we do should reflect that and we should always do things to the best of our abilities. Now, I constantly remind myself to be the best person that I can be and my hope is that you would do the same, too. **Our lives should not be lived to a quarter of our ability or half of our ability; we should live life according to our full ability.**

With the growth of the telecommunication industry in Africa, cellular phone usage has become popular and widespread. People are increasingly dependent on their cellphones. Besides using them for communication purposes, people use them for financial transactions, educational purposes, business purposes, as alarm clocks, for entertainment, and so on. It is also common to find all the major cellphone brands from around the world all over Africa, such as Apple, BlackBerry, and Motorola.

Imagine if Apple said, "From this day forward, we will make phones that are just good enough to last for a day, or maybe a week." Would you be eager to purchase a phone like that? Imagine if BlackBerry also said, "Let's manufacture a mediocre phone." Nobody would get excited about owning a phone like that. The competition would easily crush these companies with better phones and would take over the market.

If you don't want to own a phone like that, then why would you desire to be mediocre? Why would you be comfortable achieving "just okay" results? Why are you only doing the minimum that is required of you? Why do you not give your best every time? If you continue being mediocre, you too will get crushed in the marketplace. People will beat you to the best jobs, the best deals, and the best opportunities.

I doubt that most people get up in the morning and say, "I hope I have a mediocre day today." But many still go on to have mediocre days. If people are not saying this to themselves, then why are they doing mediocre things and seeking mediocre results? They are comfortable operating at this level of mediocrity because they do not have to try too hard to get there or maintain a level of mediocrity. This is one of the reasons why mediocrity is so deceiving. Being that it is the middle ground between good and bad, it easy for people to accept it as their standard of practice. They can look at what they've done and say, "It's not too bad," or "It's good enough," when they are indeed lying to themselves. Many people who operate at this level will not be successful in the things they want until they change, because mediocrity itself is an enemy of success. **Mediocrity is bad and excellence should always be your standard, not mediocrity.** Don't settle for average or just being okay; push yourself to do your very best.

Another reason people are this way is because they have become stuck in a culture of mediocrity and it becomes a habit. They surround themselves with other mediocre people who don't know any different. They encourage this continued mediocrity, building a culture of mediocrity without even knowing it. As a result of this culture, people are now accustomed to accepting mediocrity. Even the government is mediocre in their governance and people accept it just the way it is. It is time to break free from this culture of mediocrity. It is time to set a new tone for living. It is time to chart a new course and a new standard for everyone to live by.

Commonly, service workers such as mechanics and bricklayers try to push their mediocrity on people for whom they perform a service. After doing mediocre work, they tell the customer that he or she should accept the work they have done. Even when it is clear that the right thing to do is to try and fix the situation or make it better, they instead continue to tell the customer not to worry too much about their mediocre work since "it is not that bad." It is important to communicate your standards to these providers upfront. Let them know what your standards are and if they are unable to meet those standards, then you will find someone else who will. If they are serious about the job, then they will do it right; if they are not serious about it, then you can find someone else who is more serious.

Remember that if you come across someone else operating at a mediocre level, you do not have to come down to his or her level; instead, bring them up to your level of excellence. Without being disrespectful, let the person know that your standards are your standards and you are not willing to drop them. When you are clear in your communication, the person better understands your expectations and what they need to deliver, allowing everything to go much smoother.

Mediocrity is like a disease. Just as a disease starts out by affecting one area of your body and then spreads to other areas, mediocrity can do the same thing. It did that to me before I was eventually able to detect it and fight it off. The nature of mediocrity is a big reason why you want to watch it very carefully. Act quickly as soon as you see traces of mediocrity in your life; don't allow it to spread to other areas of your life.

Success works in the same way, too. Success begets more success. Once you start performing at your best in one area of your life, it spreads to other areas. As you get the results you want, the desire for more begins to grow. As it grows, you want to experience it more and that desire helps push you toward achieving it in other areas of your life.

The standards you set for yourself are very important. Setting low standards means you will only put in enough effort to achieve those low standards. Setting high standards will push you to put in a higher level of effort. Let the very best be your benchmark. In the same way, do not use other mediocre people as your role models; use people of excellence instead, people whose lives have significance and something you aspire toward. These are also people who have admirable qualities and whose lives and actions bring out the best in you, encouraging you to do more.

Mediocrity is infectious and easy to pick up from others around you who operate at a mediocre level. Their influence could start out very subtle and go easily unnoticed until it starts showing up in different areas of your life. It's important to be careful about the people you surround yourself with. Some people might have a problem with mediocrity and not even realize that they do. It takes a little bit of introspection and honesty with oneself to see and acknowledge that the problem exists. Also, when you see elements of mediocrity in others, do not encourage them by telling them that what they have done is okay or that they do not have to do more. Even when that is the way they have always acted or done things, do not encourage them to continue to do things that way. Challenge them to do better as you challenge yourself in the same way.

In the long run, mediocrity is more expensive than excellence. Let us say, for example, you are looking to construct something. If you construct a mediocre building or a mediocre road, it will cost you more time, more effort, more resources, and more money to fix future problems. If you had just done it excellently the first time around, you would only have had to do it once.

Do not underestimate your capabilities. You can do a lot more than you think and you do not have to live a life of mediocrity. **Mediocre effort usually yields mediocre results.** There are hardly ever any surprises with this. What you put in is what you get out. A mediocre approach is visible in your end product. Once you understand this simple philosophy, you can get to the root of the problem. When you catch yourself doing anything mediocre, stop immediately and assess what you are doing. Mediocrity is a thought process; ridding yourself of mediocrity for good starts in your head. Ask yourself, "How can I improve the situation? How can I make things better?" Once you figure out the answers to these questions, proceed down the right path; go down the path of excellence.

CHAPTER 3: ONE-MINUTE MILLIONAIRE

One-minute millionaires are always looking for shortcuts to success and riches. They are constantly fantasizing about quick ways to become millionaires. They also fantasize on a regular basis about the type of lifestyle that they would live if they were to obtain the riches they dream about. Their ultimate goal is getting rich quickly. While others are hard at work, they are thinking of ways to bypass the work that is required and instead head straight for the riches. They do not believe in working hard, being patient, or getting the proper amount of wisdom necessary to be successful. They only fixate on their quest for the shortcut to riches.

There was a certain football player who wanted to win the World Player of the Year award, which is given every year to the best football player in the whole world. Past winners include Lionel Messi, Cristiano Ronaldo, and George Weah. George Weah is the only African player to ever have won it. This football player hated practicing, so he never did it. He also did not exercise regularly so he was never in good physical shape. He did not watch his diet and ultimately became overweight. Despite all this, he still wanted to win the award.

Do you think it is possible for a person like that to be granted the award for the best player in the world? Absolutely not! If he really wants to win the award, there are certain things he would do. Players who have won the award did it through constant practice and years of devotion to working on their game. Those things cannot be done overnight and certainly not in one minute. It takes a lot of dedication, hard work, practice, and personal sacrifice to become the best football player in the world. The same goes for the one-minute millionaires looking for instant success and making quick money. In life, you must go through a process to become successful in anything that you do, including making money, which takes dedication, hard work, and personal sacrifice. It is not something that comes to you for no reason; it is something that you have to earn.

There are a few people out there who manage to become millionaires overnight by winning the lottery or receiving an inheritance of some sort from a relative. The downside to this, however, is that the odds of winning the lottery are very low and not everyone has a rich relative to inherit a substantial amount of money from. For those who manage to become rich this way, it is very common to see them easily lose all the money they obtained very quickly. Most lottery winners go on to lose all the money they won in just a few years. Even worse, a lot of them end up financially worse off than they were before they won.

This happens primarily because of something that I like to call the **character of success**. Applying this methodology is necessary to obtaining success. Even after you become successful, the character of success is still needed to sustain your success. In the same way, the character of success is needed to make money and also to keep the money that you make. Wealthy people have used it since the beginning of time to build and sustain their wealth.

The character of success is built by putting yourself through a certain process in life. There are certain life lessons that you can only learn in the struggle; these lessons cannot be learned when everything is easily handed to you. These lessons involve things like how to make and keep money and how to get the success you want in your pursuits. These lessons can only be learned when you put yourself through the proper process. As you learn and implement these lessons into your life, they begin to transform you. **When you make lots of money through your own efforts, it is because the person who you have become has been molded by a series of lessons, actions, and processes that you had to go through to get to where you are.** When you take away those lessons, actions, and processes from the equation, one may not have what it takes to handle certain situations that come up. The lessons you learn, the actions you take, and the processes you have to go through are what build the character of success. If you take the shortcuts, though, you will miss the opportunity to learn these very important lessons.

Those who go broke after winning the lottery or inheriting money do so because they have not built the character of success. Due to the nature by which the money entered their lives, they essentially skipped the process of building the character of success. If you skip the process, you might feel great about yourself in the short term because of the money you have, but in the long term, you would have been better off had you built the character of success instead of taking a shortcut. When you do not build the character of success, it leaves a void in your life that is often exposed when the application of the character of success would have gotten you through situations such as adequately managing newly found riches. It isn't until that situation occurs that people realize they are missing something in their lives.

Some people out there may say, "Let the situation happen first, then I will learn how to get out of it." Some may also say, "Let me make money first, then I will worry about learning what it takes to keep it." The unfortunate thing is that by the time the money comes, it might already be too late. The penalty of not learning the life lessons first and building the character of success before making money is greater because all the money they now have is at stake. By not learning these early lessons, they stand to lose it all. I urge you to learn the lessons first so you are prepared to sustain whatever comes your way. When you do things in proper order, the entire process becomes easier and lasts longer for you.

The majority of people who obtain something without paying the full cost do not appreciate it due to the relative ease with which they got it. They also do not appreciate it as much as the person who had to go through a lot of struggle and pain to get the same thing. **When a man goes from nothing to something through the struggle, he better appreciates his current status.** For this reason, you are far more likely to spend through money that was easily obtained than money you had to work extremely hard to get.

Having to work hard for your money as opposed to getting it easily adds an extra layer of responsibility for most people because they know that if they lose the money, they must go through everything they went through the first time to get it again. This makes them conscious of how they handle their money because they don't want to go through it all over again.

People who run into sudden riches and who later go broke do so partly because, in their minds, they are still poor. Even though their bank accounts have money in them and everything on the outside gives the appearance of being rich, these people do not feel rich inside. **Success comes from the inside out.** You must first be successful on the inside before the success is reflected on the outside. Those people who run into sudden riches only became rich because of something that happened on the outside, not the inside. When a relative hands you money, it's happening on the outside, not the inside, because it did not take an idea from the inside of your mind to make that money. So although it appears that you are now rich on the outside, your inside is still poor because it did not come up with the idea for the money.

Soon enough, your mind will push you to reflect on the outside how you feel on the inside. In order for the two to match, your poor mind will get rid of the money that you have on the outside so that it matches up with how you feel on the inside. This is why some of these people go broke. Most people who go through this are never fully aware of the reason they act this way. In a short amount of time, they are broke again and back to where their mind feels the most comfortable. If things are not right on the inside, you may lose your money. **In order to change what is on the outside, you must first change what is on the inside.** If you want to be rich on the outside, you must first be rich on the inside. It is important that the two match. If they don't, you will continue to lose what you have on the outside because you are not adequately prepared for it on the inside.

For those who lose their money quickly, there is also emotional damage that comes with going broke after once being rich. Going through a situation like that sometimes hurts much more than never being rich in the first place. Once you have tasted success and felt what it is like to be rich, the experience that you have had makes it difficult for you to go back to being content with being broke. You now know what it feels like to have the freedom and independence to buy what you like and to do what you like at any given time. The people who lose all they have no longer experience the same level of freedom and independence they had when they were rich until they change their condition.

Once people have tasted what the other side of life has to offer, their current financial situation of being broke further amplifies the hurt that they feel. Make sure you develop the character of success necessary to make and maintain whatever financial success you have. The reverse is the case for those who make money by having the character of success. Once they learn how to make money, even if they lose the money they have made, they know exactly what it takes and what they have to do to make it back.

If you fall in the category of the one-minute millionaires, you are setting yourself up to be taken advantage of. There will always be people out there with a new scheme or so-called business opportunities, waiting to pounce on people like you who are trying to make quick money. This group makes their living by taking advantage of people trying to make quick money. They would try to trick you by promising to make you rich quickly. Seeing that you are desperate for quick riches, they will use any vulnerability that you have to cheat you out of what you already have and more.

There are also people out there who run around their whole life, looking for what they regard as the "right connection." This is a person of influence who can help them get what they want. They believe that if they can just find this connection, all their problems will be solved and they will become instant millionaires. Those stuck in this mindset believe that they cannot make it until they are introduced to this person who can make all their dreams come true, going so far as to devote all their time to looking for this person.

There is nothing wrong with trying to link up with a certain connection that can help you achieve some of your goals, but **work while you wait**. Do not put your dreams on hold while waiting for this one person to show up because that person may never show and you will be left with nothing. Connections are not the only thing that can bring you success. By solely focusing on finding the right connections, you are essentially taking a gamble on everything else and you could potentially miss out on other opportunities.

If you are solely looking for connections, it clearly means that you are putting all your faith in someone else and none in your abilities or yourself. By doing this, you are essentially saying, "Without this person or connection, I cannot fulfill my dreams." You are also putting yourself in a position to be disappointed. Personally, instead of putting all my dreams, hopes, and desires into another individual's hands, I would rather take a chance on myself and my abilities.

Getting to the point of becoming rich or successful is a journey and not something that necessarily happens in an instant. Start with where you are and with what you have. From there, you can build up toward the future you want. Don't sit around, waiting for the opportunity or connection of a lifetime to bring great riches before you start doing something. Start small and work your way up from there. Commit yourself to steady progress; in due time, you will achieve the success that you seek. It takes longer to build a building with twenty floors than it takes to build a building with one floor. Work on your foundation so it is strong and take your time to build up so that whatever you build, you will keep.

CHAPTER 4: EDUCATION

I am a firm believer in education. Everyone should try to attain the highest possible level of education that they can, but not everyone has this opportunity. Regardless of your situation, you should still push yourself to get as much education as you can. But to be clear, it is not the only path to success. **Education does not guarantee success, but it gives you a good platform to succeed.** Just because you are educated doesn't mean you are guaranteed success, but if you go about it the right way, education will set you up to succeed. Some people might wonder why they should pursue it if it does not guarantee success, but then again, how many things in life are guaranteed? The answer to that is little to nothing. The fact that education gives you a platform to succeed makes it all worthwhile.

Proponents against education usually cite examples of graduates in Africa with bachelor's and master's degrees who either cannot find jobs or get low paying jobs when they do find one. They say that one needs to consider the time spent and troubles experienced at school to determine if it is all worth it. They also argue that the education you get is an investment in yourself and the main goal of every investment is to be profitable. For that reason, you have made a bad investment if the education you have isn't profitable. While there is some truth to all of this, consider this: **Even though you can take advantage of the opportunities that require no education, having an education will not stop you from taking advantage of the opportunities that require no education. The opportunities that require an education, however, can only be taken advantage of if you have an education.**

An example may help you better understand this concept: Say you are considering either being a shoe shiner or a doctor. Having an education would not stop you from being a shoe shiner, but having no education will stop you from being a doctor. This is what makes education so important. **Having an education gives you choices.** Don't limit yourself in life to only one set of opportunities. Put yourself in the very best positions to take advantage of any opportunities that come your way.

If I had a choice, however, to choose between getting an education and not getting an education, I would choose getting an education every single time because I know it is better for me in the long run. When a mechanic gets a service call to fix a car, for example, he usually doesn't know what's wrong with the car until he looks at it. Once he is able to diagnose the problem, then he can then begin to work on it. The next thing he does is reach for his tools. If he only has one or two tools in his tool box, then he is severely limited in the type of work that he can do. If he has a lot of different tools, however, he can perform several different types of work. The more tools the mechanic has, the more options he has for the type of work he can do. Education is the same; it gives you options for the type of work that you can do.

Having an education can also help you deal adequately with problems life throws at you. A good education will help you deal with problems as they arise. If a mechanic only knows how to fix bad brakes, then he can't help a person with an engine problem. In the same way, a good education comes in handy in that being knowledgeable on several matters enables you to solve different kinds of problems.

There are many views on the role that education can play in one's life; there are also many ideological battles on how education should be ranked in the order of priority in a person's life. But people fail to understand that it is not the only path to success. When I was in high school, I had the opportunity to play alongside one of the best footballers I have ever seen. This boy was amazing, a great all-around athlete. He had great speed, superb skills, and the complete package of a football star in the making. Everyone that saw him play knew that he would make a great footballer player someday.

I will never forget the day we played a rival school and he scored five goals against them. He was a terror to any defense. He, however, was challenged in his academics. His parents were so focused on his academics that they did not support his sporting abilities. He never got a chance to pursue the opportunities he had with football; the world never got to see this football star.

This story illustrates that so much talent is being wasted in Africa in sports, music, art, and other areas. Parents feel that a career based on education is much more important than a career doing anything else. But everyone has a unique gift; our duty is to develop that gift and share it with the world. Whatever talent you have, develop it and put it to use in the best way you can. The world thrives on diversity—there is no need for everybody to do the same things. I'm not saying it is wrong for parents to want their children to do better academically, but parents should not kill their children's dreams. They need to support their children to the best of their ability and provide them with an environment conducive to thriving. Instead of dismissing talent that their children have, parents should instead help them develop their talents.

Another common occurrence is where parents force their children to pursue challenging academic disciplines like medicine and engineering, contrary to the child's abilities or interest. Parents believe it sounds very good to say that their child is a doctor or an engineer as opposed to a job that is less prestigious. Even though they may mean well for their kids, parents must understand that not all children are capable of excelling in those academic disciplines. Everyone has different interests and professions that we would love to pursue. Forcing a certain profession on your child applies undue pressure that further burdens the child to perform, even though they have no genuine interest in the field. When there's no real interest in something, it's harder for anyone to perform at his or her very best level. The individual may also waste years of his or her life. There is nothing worse than pursuing a career for years and getting midway through life before realizing that it is not what you wanted to do. Imagine being fifty years old and realizing that being a doctor is not really want you wanted to do, but that you should have been a lawyer instead. Imagine what it would feel like to also know that the only reason you became a doctor was because your parents forced you. Coming to terms with something like this could result in severe emotional problems and lack of self-worth.

Imposing a career early on a child could also lead to psychological and emotional issues, where the child is unable to function appropriately in the pursuit of any other profession.

The backlash from something like this could spill over and consume other areas of the child's life. For this reason, the interests of the child should be placed above the interests of the parents. Every child should be given an orientation of the various fields and disciplines available to them. Upon determining where children's strengths and interests lie, resources and support should be diverted to that area to help them achieve their objective. To be truly successful and contented with whatever you do, you have to be passionate and driven about that cause regardless, of how naturally talented you are. **Without the drive to succeed, all the talent in the world is useless.** People need an internal drive to succeed. They have to want it for themselves and not just because they are trying to please someone else, such as their parents. **An individual's commitment to the cause is strongest when the decision comes from within.**

A common trend among parents is sending their children to expensive schools. Certain people believe that the more expensive a school is, the better the school must be. But this is wrong. A lot of these schools offer certain advantages in the form of better infrastructure, technology, and sporting facilities as compared to schools with significantly less funding, but from a purely academic standpoint, the expensive schools are not always better than the less expensive schools.

Parents must beware falling into the trap of sending their children to these schools merely as a way to boost their own social status. They have to make sure that the child's best interest is always considered. Irrespective of how cheap or expensive a school is, nothing can replace the personal will and drive of the child to succeed at school. A child not driven to succeed will not succeed, regardless of what school the child is in. Also, nothing can replace giving a child the proper amount of attention to develop academic excellence. Parents must help their children accomplish this by building a strong foundation for the child. It is not up to teachers or a school to solely manage a child's education; it is the parents' responsibility first.

Since building a strong foundation during the early childhood years is important, parents who are academically able should spend time working with their children on schoolwork. When you show interest in your child's work, the child understands how important the work is and is therefore more likely to take schoolwork seriously. Help the child make a habit of doing schoolwork outside of the classroom, as this can stay with a child forever. It's important to start reinforcing good habits early. If you examine your life and your habits as they are today, you will discover you still do certain things the same way since your childhood.

     Help your child develop positive habits through repetition and positive reinforcement. Have your child repeat the action that you want to see over and over again till it becomes a habit. Form good habits through positive reinforcement by rewarding your child every time he or she does what you would like to see more of. Helping your child build positive habits and skills in their younger years benefits them for the rest of their lives.

     When most people think of education, they think of a classroom setting. But education doesn't always have to be formal. Education can happen anywhere: at home, at work, or even outdoors. There are no confines to where and how you can be educated. Do whatever you can to get as much education as possible. It will increase your awareness and your capability to be more than you currently are. Success is a numbers game. The more doors you can open for yourself, the more your chances of success go up. Do the right things to increase your chances for success. Put yourself in the right positions to take advantage of opportunities when they arise.

CHAPTER 5: PERSONAL DEVELOPMENT

To progress in life, I don't focus on how much I have done but on how much I have yet to do.

Like the saying goes, if you are not growing, you are dying. Growth is one of our main objectives in life, and not just physical growth in the sense of growing taller or stronger, but growth in every area of life, be it emotional, mental, spiritual, or professional. Personal development is also an essential part of growth that involves self-development through various activities. This type of growth requires effort; it does not happen automatically. The wonderful thing about personal development is that you have the power to grow in any direction you want. There is also no limit to how much you can grow, which means you can continue to grow throughout your life.

When engaging in the process of personal development, grow every day in every way that you can. Do not think of yourself as a finished product; instead, constantly strive to get better and better. Nothing should stop you from continuing to grow or from continuing to engage yourself in the personal development process. It doesn't matter what family you were born into or what position your parents occupy in the society; nothing should stop you from developing yourself. The only person that can stop you *is* you. You have a duty to yourself to pursue your personal development; if you do so, then no one, not even yourself, can hold you back. No matter where you are in the personal development process, remember: Everyone has to start from somewhere. Begin with where you are and then develop yourself from there.

A chair is more valuable than a piece of wood; people are willing to pay more for a chair than they are for the same piece of wood from which it was made. Through an individual's labor and efforts, the piece of wood was transformed into a chair. In the same way, you can transform yourself through the process of personal development. By transforming yourself, you can essentially increase your value; by adding more value to your life, you increase your capacity to earn more money and people are willing to pay you more for your increased value.

If you want to earn a certain amount of money, develop yourself into the person who is worth being paid that amount of money. One of the ways to develop yourself is to increase your learning. **The amount of your learning and the amount of your earning go hand in hand.** If you want your income to grow, you have to grow as a person, too.

The desire to pursue the process of personal development to add value to your life must be strong and definite so you can press on, irrespective of any obstacles. The desire must be definite in its application so it can be applied exactly how and where it is needed to get the right results. Apply this desire to the area of your life that needs development and affects your value. This process will require a lot of time and effort for it to be a success.

If you are currently employed, it is your responsibility to work on your personal development. Look for opportunities to grow yourself; don't rely on your employer to provide you with all the opportunities. Naturally, the longer you perform the same duties at your job, the better you get at it. However, don't stop there. Let's say, for example, you have a construction job as a bricklayer. As you do this job over and over again, over time you become better at laying bricks through repetition and able to do it faster. Personal development goes beyond all that; it is deliberate and intentional. You must develop new skills and learn new things beyond what naturally comes by doing the same job repeatedly over a period of time.

One of the secrets to advancing in any job is to make yourself more valuable to your employer than what your position calls for. Using the example of the bricklayer, don't just learn how to lay bricks; learn other tasks and skills associated with that job, but outside of the work that you normally do. Your ability to do this shows your employer that you are capable of doing more and that you are worthy of promotion. Complete job-related professional certifications or courses to help you stand out as an employee. When you do this, both current and prospective employers see it as a positive and will look to you as an individual who is committed to growth.

Put together a personal development plan for yourself to outline what your goals are and how you plan to achieve them. When it comes to creating a personal development plan, think in terms of where you currently are and where you want to be in the future. What would you like to achieve? What type of position would you like to have? What kind of income would you like to make? Once you have a clear picture of what this looks like, the next thing is to determine what steps to take to accomplish those personal development goals.

Know that this calls for a level of sacrifice from you. **There is no progress or accomplishment without sacrifice.** Be prepared to sacrifice certain things to get the results that you want. Some examples include taking a course or attending a seminar to develop yourself instead of spending money on new clothes. Making a sacrifice could also mean spending money to buy a book that would help in your personal development instead of spending it on a new pair of shoes. It could also mean spending time on beneficial activities instead of spending your time unwisely.

With a personal development plan in place, you are more likely to keep yourself active in the personal development process. Then you know exactly what you need to do at each point in time. This serves as a guide and makes it easier for you to do those things. Measure your progress with each step you take throughout the process; by so doing, you can keep yourself on track toward achieving your personal development goals.

A carefully developed and executed personal development plan will help you get more out of yourself and helps set up the right expectations for you to follow. This makes for a more efficient process because it cuts straight to the activities that give you the best opportunity for growth by bypassing all the other activities that would just have wasted your time. You are, in essence, increasing your productivity.

Aside from reading books, pursuing a higher level of education, and taking courses and certifications related to your profession, there are other things that you can do to grow. First, you must realize there is no growth without discontent. **You**

must have a level of discontent to feel the urge to want to grow. If you are content with your situation, then you will not feel the need to grow or develop yourself. To develop yourself, you have to go beyond just being comfortable; you have to want more for yourself and be ready to do what it takes. In so doing, you will pay more attention to opportunities to develop yourself.

Role models are a good way to develop yourself. These are people you've identified as exhibiting qualities that you admire. Do your research on them: Find out what books they read, where they went to school and the type of education they have, what they do differently in their lives, how they developed the qualities that you admire. Find out all you can about them. If your role model is easily accessible to you, you can personally ask these questions. If this is not the case, find out what you can from someone else who knows the individual really well. You can also find good information through trustworthy sources on the Internet and from reputable publications.

Don't forget to challenge yourself: Surround yourself with people who make you think differently for the better, people who, either through their deeds or their words, challenge you to push yourself. Challenge yourself in ways that would grow and develop you into the person that you want to be. Stay determined and see yourself through the challenges you come up against; you will achieve the things you set out to do.

You can develop yourself through the pursuit of excellence. By being dedicated to mastering your craft, you can achieve excellence; commit yourself to being the best. The very best people in any chosen field always find ways to get better and better. A top sprinter, for example, continuously works on speed, technique, and endurance to help him or her improve performance. A top teacher is always learning more and finding efficient ways to teach and help students understand things better. Commit yourself to doing the same.

Personal development is about investing in *you*; just as you would in a business or idea, you should also invest in yourself. A percentage of the income that you make should go back into self-investment. There was a time in my life that I used to run from problems, but later on in life, I realized that you cannot avoid them. As humans, we are bound to run into problems from time to time. **Don't run away from problems; instead, develop yourself so much that no matter what problem you encounter, you will have what it takes to overcome it.** When you develop yourself the right way, the problems that troubled you in the past become non-issues.

The key to your personal development lies in your daily routine. Do something every day to improve yourself. Even when you're not sure of what to do, come up with new ideas to develop yourself. The answers you get from asking yourself the right questions will guide you. Base these questions on your individual situation and the type of results that you want. Pay close attention to the answers that come from within. Ask yourself: What can I do today to _____? (Fill in the blank with the desired result.) Below are some examples:

What can I do today to grow myself?
What can I do today to help me get my dream job?
What can I do today to help me get the type of income I want?
What can I do today to help me become a better person?

You cannot afford to be casual with this personal development process, or make up excuses for not doing it such as being too busy or that today is not a good day. Put time into growing yourself and realize that every day is a good day to work toward your personal development. As you do this, both your income and your abilities will grow. There are also health benefits to the process. Continuously engaging yourself in self-development helps keep your mind active, and those who do so through their old age tend to live longer. A lot of people are afraid to change. But it is in your best interest to make changes by engaging in the process of self-development. Be mindful of the fact that what you settle for in life is often what you get out of it. If you want to do better for yourself, then you have to change your situation and changing your situation begins with developing yourself.

LESSON II: EMPOWERMENT

You were made for far more than what you currently do. What you are today is not the best that you can be. You have greatness in you. Irrespective of your past, there is a better future ahead of you. Whatever happened to you in the past has already happened and cannot be changed. Start looking forward, not backward. Make a conscious decision that your future will be better than your past. No matter your situation or your past, you have the opportunity to change your story for the better, starting today.

You have a choice in how you view and interpret your life. You can either look at the problems you come across as opportunities or concede to being defeated by them. Either way, the choice is yours. Seeing your problems as opportunities allows you to look at things differently, giving you a fresh perspective so you can see the good in situations that you would not otherwise see. When you concede to only seeing problems, that is all you will see; but if you look for the good in something, then you will see it for that.

We do not get to choose how we start out in life. We do not get to choose the day we are born or the family we are born into, what we are named at birth, what country we are born in, and we do not get to choose our ancestry. All these things are predetermined by a higher power. By the time you are old enough to start making decisions for yourself, a lot of things in your life are already in place. It's important, therefore, that you focus on the future, the only thing that you can change.

It is not about where you start in life, but about how you finish. In the same way, it is not so much about what life hands you, but what you do with what you get. It is very possible to make something out of nothing. Like the saying goes, if life hands you lemons, make lemonade. And after you make lemonade, plant the seeds from the lemons that life handed you and grow more lemons out of it. This is the way I see life. Take advantage of every opportunity you come across and use them to create more opportunities. Whatever your circumstances, you will make adjustments along the way to accomplish what you want.

Lots of people started poorly in life, but were able to turn things around for the better. There are people who were born into poverty, but eventually became rich. There are people who were born with limited opportunities, but could still carve a way for themselves. There are some who were told they would never make anything good out of their lives; they proved those people wrong. There are orphans who had no family members to help them out, but still went on to live successful lives. There are people who struggled with education in their early years, but still went on to succeed academically and become leaders in their field. No matter what your condition is, your best is still in front of you. Stop thinking that you are stuck wherever you are and start believing you can change your situation.

Empowerment is all about taking charge of your life and your actions. It is about believing in your capabilities and knowing that you have immense possibilities in front of you. An empowered individual can always change a victim story to a victory story. Empowerment is taking full responsibility of your life and knowing that you play a big part in it. Empowerment means knowing you no longer have to blame other people or things for your own problems. You have what it takes to overcome any problems you face; stay strong so you can tap into the resources that you need to succeed. We complain about everything: weather, the government, teachers, textbooks, roads, messengers, and even the message. It is time to do something constructive instead of complaining. Use the energy and time that you spend complaining to do something about your present condition.

Most people think very lowly of themselves, and as a result, they set low standards for their quality of life, living conditions, education, earning ability, and for their health. They believe they cannot do better. Reexamine your standards and raise them. Do not be discouraged if you don't reach these higher standards immediately. Hang in there; keep pushing yourself. When you do reach them, raise them again and immediately begin reaching for the new standards.

Most people also believe they are unimportant and insignificant compared to other people around them. This may be because other people are richer, more educated, or come from more prominent families. Whatever the other person's situation is, do not let it make you feel insignificant. You are special in your own way; you just have to discover what is special about *you*. Only then can you begin to make important contributions and express yourself to the degree that you were meant to. Remember, you matter. You are important.

You have the power to change your life at this very moment. You have the power in you to live a rich and wonderful life. You are more powerful than the overwhelming circumstances that you find yourself in. Nothing will change in your life until you want it to. You have to decide to make a change and you have to make that decision quickly. **In the words of Albert Einstein, "The definition of insanity is doing the same thing over and over again and expecting different results."** It's not going to happen. If you keep doing the same thing you have always done, you will keep getting the same results that you have always gotten. Ask yourself: Am I happy with the results in my life currently? Are you always wanting better for yourself? Do you find yourself not able to get the right kind of grades in school? If so, it is time to try things differently. Your results can change tremendously by trying a different approach. Start by changing one thing and see how it affects your results. If you don't get the results you want, try something else to change your results. From there, you can make decisions around which direction you should go.

Nobody should want change in your life more than you do. Not your parents, friends, religious leader, teacher, or anybody else. People can give you ideas and advice, but true motivation for action must come from inside. You have to step up and take control of your situation. Challenge yourself to make the change you want to see in your life. Your motivation must be real and important to generate the right level of desire for action.

Whenever you are going through a challenging situation, remember that there are lessons to learn from it. Pay attention to the lessons that come with those experiences and learn how to overcome a challenging situation or how to completely avoid it the next time. Ask yourself, "How can I empower myself in this situation? How can I grow from this?" Take good notes of your responses and the lessons you learn, using them to your advantage. If those challenging situations get the best of you, remember: It is not over yet. You have plenty left in you to overcome it. No matter your situation or circumstances, stand tall and remember that you are made for more.

CHAPTER 6: POVERTY

It takes nothing to stay in poverty, but everything to break free from it.

After a careful analysis of the major plights of the average African, I have come to the conclusion that the underlying problem is poverty. If you consider such problems as bad government, political unrest, war, lack of education, limited access to quality health care, affordability of health care, corruption, access to clean water, and so on, you'll realize that all these problems are related to poverty. By educating the African populace on how to get out of poverty, we will be, in essence, fixing a lot of problems at once. The high mortality rates and the low quality of life linked to poverty are far too concerning to ignore. We must act and do something to decrease the level of poverty. The people need solutions.

Poverty hinders you from achieving your full potential. It holds you back from being the person you are capable of becoming. When you are in poverty, it's even more challenging to get the right type of education or to develop yourself, but it is not impossible. When you are able to operate at your full potential, everyone benefits and you are in a position to help others. When you can't, the world misses out on you and what you could have offered.

Why do people stay in poverty? Is it because they are bad people? Is it because they don't work hard enough? Is it because there is not enough money in the world to go around for everyone? The answer to the last question is no. In fact, there is enough money and resources in the world for everyone to share. The problem lies, in part, with the approach each person takes in tapping into what's available.

Somewhere in a remote African village, there is a woman by the name of Agu. She is fifty-six years old and gathers and sells firewood for a living. She has been doing this job every day for the last twenty-seven years since her husband passed away. Agu is well loved in her village because she is a genuinely good person. She is kind to people and always available to help others when she can. Every day, at 5 a.m., Agu sets out into the forest to gather firewood. Armed with nothing but a machete, or cutlass, as it is known in parts of Africa, she works hard at chopping down wood. Her back aches from having to bend over to chop down wood as she has done for so many years. The palms of her hands are bruised and bloody with wood splinters from the grip of the machete and from gathering the firewood.

The long hours of work has taking a toll on her body, but Agu cannot afford to get the medical attention she needs because she is unable to afford it. She walks with a limp as a result of pain in one of her legs, and it is clear to see that, physically, Agu's best days are behind her if she does not get medical attention. When the sun sets, Agu loads the wood on her head and heads home to the village before it gets too dark. On Saturdays, she sells her firewood at the market. Over the years, she has learned that this allows her to make a higher profit by selling directly to her customers without going through anyone else. But even then she only makes a small amount of money, about five American dollars, for a week's worth of gruesome work. Agu has been working continuously for the last twenty-seven years and, despite this, she remains in poverty.

There is no doubt that Agu works hard and she's a good person. Agu's problem is not a lack of effort or a lack of hard work; the problem lies with the capacity of the work she does. Agu could gather wood for the rest of her life in the same manner that she has always done and she would never be able to lift herself out of poverty. She has maximized the capacity of the job she is doing based on the approach she takes toward her job. The thought pattern for people in situations like hers is that if they could only work much harder, then and only then would they be able to rise from poverty. When you work on something that only has the capacity to make you $5, it does not matter how much harder you work—the most you will make is $5.

Agu can lift herself out of poverty by changing the approach to her job. For example, Agu is limited in the amount of firewood she can gather by herself each day. By getting help, she could gather more firewood to sell. Also, Agu brings home only the amount of firewood that she can transport on her head each day. By finding an alternative mode of transportation, she could bring more firewood to the village to sell. The biggest difference Agu can make is if she applies the same work ethic she uses to work now to a job that has a higher capacity to earn her more money. Instead of working on something that only has the capacity to earn $5, she can apply the same work ethic to something that has the capacity to earn her $100.

The capacity of what you apply yourself to and the approach you take toward it matters. The issue of capacity applies to any type of work and to anybody. It does not matter if you are a farmer, electrician, banker, builder, bus driver, engineer, or in any other profession—there is a certain level of capacity to whatever you do. Keeping this in mind will help you make life decisions. Lots of people out there work from sunrise to sunset, yet still remain poor. Just like Agu, the problem has nothing to do with their work ethic, but rather how and at what they are working hard toward.

The issue of *individual* capacity is the reason why a doctor earns more money than a bricklayer earns. Both professions require different levels of expertise, but they also offer a difference in value to those they serve. They do their jobs and get paid according to their individual capacity. Since you make money according to your individual capacity, it is therefore important for you to raise your capacity to make more money. As you raise your individual capacity, your level of expertise increases and the value you offer also increases. Poverty is not an everlasting condition; it is something you can rise from. By taking the right steps to learn new skills, educate yourself and increase your capacity, you can fight your way out of poverty.

Many rich people today started out poor, but through their own deliberate effort, they overcame poverty. They never accepted it, seeing it only as a temporary situation. They knew that if they worked hard to achieve their personal goals, they could claw their way out of poverty. And they succeeded; they were able to improve themselves and enjoy a better quality of life.

Don't believe those who say that only rich people or the children of the rich have a chance at success. A good example that disputes this misconception is my father. He was born in a village far away from the city to a poor family. The major occupation in his village was farming; not a lot of people made it out of that lifestyle. But he believed there was more in life for him. Despite starting out late, he was admitted into a secondary school far away from his village. Through hard work and dedication, he became an outstanding scholar and a great athlete, too, going on to break and set many school records in track. He was offered scholarships to various universities around the world and even was accepted into an ivy league university in the United States, an incredibly impressive feat for anyone.

The only thing he had to do was get on a plane to America to start his new life. Unfortunately, due to his financial condition, he could not afford the flight, and just like that, the dream was dead. He missed out on a wonderful opportunity to attend a university where he could have studied with some of the brightest students in the world.

A setback like this could have easily destroyed anyone, but he never gave up on life. When one path didn't work, he simply followed another. He chose to study at a Nigerian university where he was also offered a scholarship that helped pay his way through school. At one point in his career, he was chosen to represent Nigeria in the track and field events in the 1968 Summer Olympic Games in Mexico. But the date of the Olympic Games clashed with a major exam he had to take to further his education. He chose to take the exam and pursue his goal of becoming an engineer. So again, he faced another setback. Back in those days, a career as an athlete in Nigeria was not as promising and rewarding as it is today. He made the choice that he felt was the best for him in the long term. Despite forgoing the Olympic Games, his decision paid off: My father went on to have a very successful and accomplished career as an engineer, reaching the highest position possible within his organization as CEO.

The moral of this story is that you can make it, as long as you keep pushing forward, regardless of what setbacks you face. The drive to succeed far outweighs any talent that you might have. **Without the drive to succeed, all the talent in the world is useless.** Your talent may open doors for you, but you must take advantage of those opportunities by being the best that you can be. As a parent, you can also do the same for your children by encouraging and supporting them to be their very best. My dad worked hard to be the very best he could be, and as a parent, he did the exact same thing for me. For that reason, I have the opportunity to write this book.

There are countless success stories of people who had nothing when starting out in life, but, through hard work and determination, they became successful. This could be your story, too, regardless of the obstacles you currently face or will face down the road. Poverty is like a giant spider web that keeps you trapped: it is very sticky and is difficult to get out of once you fall prey to it. To break free and be successful, you must work hard and be determined.

My father encountered many roadblocks along the way, but he never let them stop him. To him, they were nothing but obstacles to his success that may have slowed him down, but he never let them stop him from achieving his dreams. Like every other obstacle in life, part of what is required of you to overcome it is to persevere, regardless of what stands in your way. With time, you will get to your intended destination.

The more people who can lift themselves out of poverty, the better it is for others. Their ability to do this represents possibilities for others, letting others know that they can also make it out of poverty. If anyone in your country, state, or village can become wealthy, you can do it, too. Those with success stories can give you hope and serve as a goal toward which you can aspire. Many remain in poverty today because they feel hopeless. They believe it's impossible to rise above it. But if you believe it is possible, you are already one step closer toward doing it. The opportunities are out there; you just have to learn to recognize and take advantage of them.

Having lots of people who have made their way out of poverty also helps eliminate the problem of dependency in Africa. In Africa, when one family member makes it, all the other family members surround that one person and live off him or her. Having to be responsible for all of your extended family members who are counting on you for financial support can be very demanding. It puts a lot of weight on your shoulders, easily leading to stress, which can sometimes drag down your work performance. It pays to have as many people as possible carrying their own weight.

Gratitude, or being thankful for what you already have, is a wonderful thing to adopt in your life. For someone that is poor, it can be difficult to get in the mood to give thanks for anything. The natural tendency for those who do not have a lot is to complain about the things they do not have. If you are in this situation, try something different: Be thankful for the things that you *do* have. There is power in having gratitude and giving thanks for what you have; it attracts *more* to you. If you are not sure of what to be thankful for, do a thorough examination of your life and think about the good things about it. There is bound to be something for which you are grateful. For one thing, you still have life. Develop a habit of being grateful and thankful for everything good in your life, and you'll find you are actually opening the door for more good to come into your life.

Even though things may feel tough right now, believe that you can get through it. We live in a world of abundance; whatever you need is somewhere out there. It is just a matter of finding a way to tap into the abundance, which may mean changing the approach you currently take or changing your focus to a completely new direction. Take a good look at the capacity of what you are doing and your own individual capacity to make sure that they match your expectations. If they don't, make the changes required of you. Your ability to access tapping into the abundance available to you grows as your capacity grows. You are worthy of living a good life that is meant for everyone. Go out and make these changes so you can tap into the abundance that is out there for you.

CHAPTER 7: ENTREPRENEURSHIP

I am always thinking of new ideas...
I am constantly exploring new opportunities...
I am driven by the urge to achieve...
I am an entrepreneur.

It is a known fact that the government does not do enough for its people in the way of creating jobs and opportunities. The simple solution to this: Create your own opportunities. Although the thought of doing this might initially sound difficult to you, I will go in more detail on how it can be accomplished. First, let's start off with who an entrepreneur is: An entrepreneur is a person who organizes and operates a business with a certain amount of risk in the expectation of gaining profit.

I strongly believe there are more business and growth opportunities in Africa at this time than anywhere else in the world. Africa is regarded as a developing continent; the process of development brings with it lots of opportunities, and only those prepared to look for these opportunities can take advantage of them and build businesses to help them succeed financially.

The general school of thought is that you need a lot of money to start a business, but you really don't. Just start small and slowly grow the business with the profits obtained from it. With time and by taking the right steps, your small business will become a big business.

Deciding what business to start could be difficult, but if you observe your environment well enough and put some thought into it, the ideas will flow. Often, it does not have to be something new. You could improve on something that already exists by making it cheaper, easier to operate, or taking it to places where it is currently not available. You could also start a business based on an "old thing" that everyone else is doing. All you have to do is find a way to do it better than everyone else. If you can beat the competition, you will be in business.

Offer better quality products or a better service to your customers than your competitors can. Learn to do things faster or offer a better-quality product than your competitors. The goal is to find a winning edge that sets you apart from others and keeps customers coming back.

An entrepreneur also solves problems for others. As a problem solver, your business can provide solutions to the problems you come across. If you are facing particular problem, others are probably facing the same problems, such as traveling, feeding, living, or housing. If you can find a solution to these problems, there is bound to be someone else that would be interested in it. You just have to find that person and connect them with your solution.

Thinking of an entrepreneur as a problem solver allows you to see opportunities that were not previously visible. If an entrepreneur is a problem solver, then Africa is an entrepreneur's dream. With all the frequently talked-about problems that exist in Africa, there is a lot of work available to keep an entrepreneur busy. There are opportunities just waiting for the right person to come along and take advantage of them. When you offer solutions to problems, you are not only helping yourself, but also helping the people around you.

As an entrepreneur, you must give yourself as much exposure as you can because it helps you identify opportunities better. **An informed mind can recognize opportunities where others cannot.** It is the same way a trained artist and a regular person can look at the same painting but see it differently. An artist, due to training, can appreciate art in ways that others cannot see. By exposing yourself to opportunities, you can see more opportunities in life, just like an artist sees details in a painting. The more exposure you get, the more aware you become. You can look at things more critically to see the opportunities that lie within them. **You see things not for what they are, but for what they could be.** The ability to see potential is an important edge that sets an entrepreneur apart.

Most people believe they have to know everything about a business before starting one. They also believe they have to learn and perfect every skill required for the business before starting it, but this is incorrect. Having all these things down before starting your business gives you a better chance of building a successful business, but it is not an absolute requirement. As an entrepreneur, you don't have to know it all;

instead, surround yourself with the right people and structure, and you'll find success. You should learn as much as you can about the business, but if you keep waiting till you know everything, you will never start it.

By overanalyzing every detail before starting your business, you could encounter analysis paralysis. This is when you overanalyze or overthink something so much that it bogs you down, and you eventually do nothing. If you never get to the point of starting the business, then you don't stand a chance of succeeding in that business. Remember that you can develop any skill that is required for any job; all that is required is your devotion to learning and practicing that skill. Some people are naturally talented, and then there are others who are quick at grasping certain skills. Even if you don't fall into either of those categories, you can still learn what is required of you.

Entrepreneurs are thinkers, especially when it comes to providing a service or product. **Never underestimate the power of thought; it is the greatest path to discovery.** As an entrepreneur, you should constantly think and explore new ideas and opportunities that you could potentially turn into a business. The simplest of ideas could lead to more wealth than you have ever dreamed of. A lot of people are misled into thinking they need sophisticated, outrageous ideas to start a business, but most times, this is not the case. All you need is an idea that is just good enough to take off. The great ideas are in you; I know they are. You just have to think, identify them, and then bring the ideas to life.

Most successful entrepreneurs share a high level of passion and drive to succeed. They believe strongly in what they do and they are ready to do whatever it takes to get the desired results. This is a core requirement for success, not just in business, but in everything. The burning desire to succeed is the reason why business owners continue to work hard, irrespective of whether or not the business is doing well. Don't let anyone kill your drive to succeed. Many will try to discourage you; even the people closest to you, like your family and loved ones who don't understand, will try as well. You cannot give in to them. Your friends will tell you that you're wasting your time; your wife or husband will tell you that your product or service is not good enough; family members will tell you that you are not making any money. Remember that the desire to be successful is the most important part of running a business. Once this fades away, so will your business.

Protect your passion for your business and hold it dearly to you. Challenges along the way will push you to the edge and make you want to quit, but you cannot concede. Keep your eyes on the end goal and continue to push, irrespective of your current situation. This is an important part of what it takes to be a successful entrepreneur, where you see something that others don't and you are committed to the cause even when they don't understand what you're doing. You have to remind them that this is why *you* are taking the risk with the business, and not them. When you do become successful, they will finally understand your commitment.

You can easily turn a hobby or something that bring you joy into a business. In fact, this is one of the easiest ways to maintain a passion for your business. When you do something that brings you joy or that you are passionate about as a business, it becomes easy for you to work long hours on it, to go the extra mile for your business, to refuse to quit when the going gets tough because you love what you do. You don't feel stressed on the job because it's something you enjoy. You also look forward to going to work every day, enjoy unlike the millions of people out there who only show up to their job because they get paid for doing so. If you are in a business that you are passionate about, your reason for doing it is bigger than just money.

Networking is also a vital part of running a business. It's about developing contacts and access to a group of people who can influence the outcome of your business. The more people you have in your network, the greater the amount of access you have. Take care with how you handle relationships you build with friends and family along the way. Nobody knows where anyone will end up. That person that you think is insignificant today could be someone important tomorrow. They could be so important that they might someday be the person that makes a big decision concerning your business or life. Everybody is important; never look down on anyone or discount anyone as too small. When networking, the right approach isn't to only think of what you can get from someone else, but how you can both benefit from your relationship together. Often, go as far as helping the other person, even though you will not necessarily get anything back for what you are doing.

The type of person you are is usually reflected in your business. **To improve your business, first improve yourself.** If you are lazy person, it will be visible in your business. If you are a wicked person, it will be visible in your business. If you are a person who does not follow the rules, it will be visible in your business. If you want to correct these things in your business, you must first correct them in your personal life. This also applies to schoolwork, farm work, homework, or working for an employer. This is all part of self-development: By encouraging you to improve yourself, you win doubly because you become a better person *and* your business also gets better.

If you are going to be in business, you must learn about money: how it works, how it flows, and how to put it to work for you. You need at least a basic level of understanding accounting to accurately keep records and properly track your inventory. If you have no system for this, your business will not thrive as it should. If you are not good at accounting, hire someone who can do it with you. Even after hiring someone, you should still have a general understanding of accounting because it's easier for you to understand what the other person is telling you and you can make sure that the person is helping you in business-related matters.

I've mentioned that first you work for money and then you have money work for you. Running a business is one of the ways of having money work for you. By putting your money into a business, money will be generated for you. This does not happen automatically without any effort on your part; **you have to work on the business first before it works for you**. Be prepared for the ups and downs, as businesses work in cycles. There will be times when everything would be going great, and also times when things are not so great. It is all part of running a business.

As an entrepreneur, do not be scared to dream. Even when people think your dream sounds crazy and impossible, hold on to your dream anyway. Before many inventions were created, it was crazy to think that they would work, like a large ship that could float on water without sinking. It was crazy and impossible to think that a plane, as heavy as it is, could fly in the air without immediately dropping to the ground. Before the telephone, it was crazy to think you could talk to someone in a place that was far away from where you were without having to be physically in front of that person. Regardless of how crazy and impossible all these things once sounded, they were done only because someone believed they were possible. The same goes for whatever idea or dream that you have today. It might sound impossible now, but that is only because people have yet to see it. When you create it, then they will know that it was possible all along.

CHAPTER 8: MINDSET

The significant problems we have cannot be solved at the same level of thinking with which we created them.
—Albert Einstein

The mind is a powerful thing. It is therefore unfortunate that most people go through life only using a fraction of what the mind is capable of doing. Their inability to tap into the immense possibilities of the mind is something I consider a big waste of human potential. There is so much more you can do with your mind if you know how to apply it correctly. In this chapter, we will go over the mind, its potential, and how to properly apply it to greatly improve your life.

The mind constantly generates thoughts that guide every decision and action you take. Where you are today are due to the thoughts that go through your mind. For example, you made a decision to get up from bed this morning based on your thoughts. You also decided whether or not to leave the house based on thoughts. Before coming to a final decision, you thought about the different options that you had, after which you made a decision and followed through. The accumulation of the decisions that you have made in life is what brought you exactly to where you are at this moment.

As humans, we are designed to think, and what we think about shapes our lives. There is no limit to how broadly we can think, but over time, we have limited ourselves in our thinking. A lot of people fall into the category of putting limits on themselves, but there is still hope for them to make a change. Regardless of how much you have limited your mind in the past, you can still expand it. The mind is just like a muscle—the more you exercise it, the stronger it gets and the more it can expand. If you don't use it, it doesn't get stronger or expand. It is therefore important that you constantly push the limits of your mind so you can get more out of it. Your mind has no bounds and that is exactly how you should treat it.

One way to expand your mind is to have high expectations for yourself. This forces your mind to be more than it currently is by coming up with new thoughts and ideas on how to meet the expectations you have set for yourself. This is a continuous process; as long as you keep working toward the expectations, your mind will continue to generate different ideas for you to meet those expectations. The mind is a wonderful thing to have working for you. A well-conditioned mind will always help you live up to your own expectations.

Your mindset today is not something that you developed overnight. It's been shaped over time, based on the various life experiences you've had right from childhood. These experiences have either limited, developed, or strengthened your mindset. As a child, a lot of limits were put on what you could do or not do. You were told that you could touch certain things but not others. You were told that certain things were possible and and others impossible. You were told what you could do and what you could not do. You also might have been told that you were not good enough to achieve something or that you could not do something because you were not from the right family. All these things have played a role in how you think today.

Throughout your life, different thoughts were planted in your head at various times. When the thoughts were planted, you made a decision whether or not to believe the thought. The decision you ultimately made helped shape your mindset. For example, if someone told you a horrible thing when you were a child, like you would never be anything in life, the first thing you'd do is think about what was said to you. Then you'd make a decision to either believe what this person said to you or not. If you believed it, you'd then consider yourself a failure and that belief would shape how you thought about yourself from that point forward. If you didn't believe it, you ignored the comment and continued on with your life.

What you accept in your mind as true becomes true to you. If someone tells you that you can't do something and you accept it as true, then it becomes difficult for you to do that thing. Whether you realize it or not, every time you make a choice, you are literally deciding what your beliefs should be. But recognize the power that lies within you: You can decide what you believe and what you don't. It is paramount that you know how important your beliefs are to you. The dominant beliefs that make up your core influence how you act on daily basis.

Avoid developing a mindset of failure that puts limits on you and affects your view of possibilities. This mindset concedes to failure even before you attempt to do anything. But as Henry Ford, the legendary industrialist, said, "Whether you think you can or you think you can't, you are right." Pay attention to your thoughts so you can eliminate those that give you undesirable results. If you eliminate thoughts of failure, consequently you'll think thoughts of success. What you are essentially doing is replacing the thoughts of the things you do not want with the thoughts of the things you actually want. Focusing on thoughts of success helps you eliminate thoughts of failure, further helping you develop a mindset of success.

With a mindset of success, you believe in what you can do and you will succeed even before you take on something new. By strengthening your success mindset, you can overcome any fear. For this reason, you are far more likely to achieve success. It also gives you the confidence you need to do a good and successful job. Therefore, approach everything you do with the expectation of success. It will completely improve your attitude and your ability to get things done.

Another type of mindset to avoid is that of poverty, which only brings about more poverty. A lot of people in a poverty mindset believe they do not deserve to be rich. They expect themselves to stay in poverty and, for that reason, they subconsciously keep themselves in poverty, even when things may be turning for the better. For example, if you like to keep your fingernails short, you will notice every time your nail grows long; your mind instantly lets you know that it is time to cut your nails. Similarly, people stuck in a poverty mindset rid themselves of any excess so they can return back to their place of comfort. You can also develop a mindset of poverty if you believe some untrue things that people say about being rich. It is common to hear that rich people are bad people or that if you become rich, people will not like you anymore. If you believe these things, you'll avoid becoming rich.

Do what you can to avoid a mindset of failure, poverty, or any other type of limiting beliefs and mindsets out there. They start out as thoughts that hold you back, and they eventually prevent you from being the best you can be. When you feel these thoughts creep into your mind, always question them: What will it cost me if I believe this thought? What kind of person will I become if I believe this thought? Will acting on this thought make me proud of myself? Questions like these help you evaluate your actions and make the right decisions. Listen and act on the answers that come to your mind; don't let your emotions get in the way of making the right decisions.

You are where you are today because of the thoughts that go through your mind. Your body, through action, follows the instructions your mind gives it. Your ability to understand this not only tells you how the mind works, but also gives you an insight into how to go about making a difference in your life. If you want to have a different life in the future, you must change your mindset. Adopt new thoughts and belief systems that steer you toward the life you want in the future. If you change your mindset, then you can change your life. As you improve the quality of the thoughts that go through your mind, you will also improve your life.

Learning to harness the power of your mind can help you get the type of results you want in life. One of the ways this can be achieved is by training your mind to think *habitual thoughts*. These are created by constantly thinking the same thoughts in your mind over and over again until those thoughts become a habit for you. You are training your mind to think a certain way by using the power of repetition. For example, if you want to create a habitual thought of success, focus on specific thoughts about success: "I am a success," "Everything I touch becomes successful," etcetera. As you focus on these thoughts, replay them in your mind till they become a part of you. As you repeat them, over time they become your habitual way of thinking, which will help you get the results you want in your life.

Understanding that whatever you feed your mind grows and expands. This is also based on the understanding that one thought leads to another. It's a domino effect: One thought causes you to think of another related thought and it goes on and on. One example is if you want to do something, but you don't know how. Start by planting a tiny seed of thought about what you want to achieve in your mind. That thought will grow and expand till it eventually leads to the thought that tells you how to do what you want to do. Pay attention to this because it can also work against you if applied incorrectly. For example, if you think angry thoughts or unforgiving thoughts about others, the end result is negative. Angry thoughts will grow till they dominate your mind and then affect things that you do negatively. Unforgiving thoughts will also expand until they dominate your mind and manifest in your actions negatively. But if you forgive someone for something they did to you, it doesn't mean you agree with what they did or believe it was right. Forgiving that person means you have chosen not to dwell on the matter anymore; you have moved on with your life.

  The power of the mind can also be harnessed by using images, which have a powerful effect on your mind. When you feed your mind images, it takes those images and develops thoughts around them. The more powerful the images are, the greater the effect they tend to have. People react differently to images they see because of each individual's own interpretation. If the images are powerful enough, they will consume your thoughts and shape your actions. When you feed your mind with the images of what you want, your mind can help you get them. For example, if you hope to one day gain admission to a certain school or work for a certain company, feed your mind with images that represent those places, and it in turn will find ways to make those goals a reality. Feeding your mind with the right images helps you begin to actualize your goals.

  From this day on, take full control of the thoughts that go through your mind. Guard your mind carefully; do not allow it to be fed with the wrong things. Close your mind to distractions and all the other things that can take you off your preferred path through life. Stay away from thoughts that are not in line with your desired results. If you identify any bad thoughts creeping around your mind, get rid of them quickly by substituting the bad thoughts with good thoughts. You can no longer afford to hold on to any thought or belief that is not serving you in the right way. Build up your mind to the point that it steadily attracts other good things to it. The mind has a powerful way of attracting things that are in harmony with it, good and bad. An abundance mindset attracts more abundance to it. A poverty mindset attracts more poverty to it. A negative mindset attracts more negativity to it. A happy mindset attracts more happiness to it and a positive mindset attracts more positivity to it.

A lot of people are guilty of not getting the most out of the power of their mind. Do not let that be you; instead, use every bit of power your mind has to offer to achieve the things you want. When you get it right first in your mind, it will be reflected in what you do. Some people say that they will start to think a certain way next week, next month, or some other time in the future, but they never get around to doing it. Start thinking the way you want to think *now*. As you start to think of great things, then you will begin to do great things. As you start to think creatively, then you will begin to create things. **In due time, you become what you think about.** There is no limit to what your mind can conceive. Use your mind to the full extent of its power. Let your creative and imaginative mind run freely; it will take you places you never dreamed of and provide breakthroughs that others once thought were impossible.

CHAPTER 9: WOMEN AND THE YOUTH

Show me the heroes that the youth of your country look up to, and I will tell you the future of your country.

For far too long, women and the youth have been shoved to the side while men continue to dominate different areas of the society. Women and the youth are not given the opportunities they deserve to prove what they are capable of doing. They are viewed as incapable by men who believe that they do not have what it takes to get the job done. While things have gotten better, Africa still has a long way to go on the issue of equality and empowerment.

The African continent now boasts a few female presidents, which is unprecedented. The progressive steps that have been taken are worthy of praise, but there is still a lot of work yet to be done. There are plenty of positions of leadership and authority on the continent with no women serving, despite the fact that lots of qualified women out there are more than capable to fulfill the positions' obligations. But they are not given a chance because of their gender.

One of the biggest reasons why a lot of African cultures do not give women the economic opportunities they deserve is a traditional way of thinking, where the woman's role solely belongs in the home. Women are only supposed to take care of the children and the affairs of the home, and nothing else. I believe in equal opportunities and not holding anyone back because of their gender. Women are equally capable of working in the government, banks, schools, and any other position of leadership. They deserve the same opportunities as men have been given.

While there are many instances of women who hold similar positions to other men, women are still not paid the same amount of money that the men receive as they are viewed as undeserving. But men and women who occupy similar positions should be paid equally. If they can both handle the same responsibilities and do the same type of work, then they shouldn't be treated differently when it comes to their pay. Everyone should be paid according to their performance, skills, education, experience, value, and every other measure of job success. No one should be getting paid or held back because of their gender.

Lawmakers and those in power must put policies in place to help women live a much more progressive life and to give them equal access to opportunities. These policies must put an end to the inequality in pay that both men and women get. These policies should also discourage any form of discrimination against women. Individuals and organizations of all kinds also have a part to play in this. They, too, can establish programs to improve the lives of women. No program or initiative is too small or too insignificant; everything from a community-based program for just a few people to a national program that includes everyone all have the ability to change lives. Every life counts and every step that is taken brings us that much closer to helping more and more people.

The women should be given a voice to speak and an opportunity to be heard. They need a platform where they can voice their concerns and express issues that are important to them. They should be encouraged to express themselves and not be condemned to a life of silence because of their views on women's empowerment. They should be provided with a medium where they can freely speak without worrying about the dangers of doing so. A lot of these women also have great ideas on how to solve the problems that they face and so therefore should be given a chance to share their ideas. The powers that be need to listen and work with women to implement the right solutions to their problems.

A lot of women's self-esteem has been shattered by years of abuse. They have endured years of being relegated to insignificance in society. It is time to help them rebuild their self-esteem. It is time for them to be acknowledged for how important they really are. Women need to be reminded that they are meaningful contributors to society, that their contributions are appreciated, and that they matter. Their self-esteem and sense of self-worth needs to be built up, not cut down. They are not inferior to men. They are just as important as any man and should be given the credit they deserve.

The youth are also deprived of opportunities in society. When you are young, so many things are held back from you until you are perceived as old enough to have them. I remember saying to myself that I could not wait to grow up so I could get all the benefits that older people get. As I got older, I could still not wait to get much older so I could get the respect and the benefits that come with old age. The older I got, the higher the age barrier rose to get the next benefit. Soon enough, I found out that this was an ever-rising age barrier. If I kept on with it, before long, I would become so old that I would wonder where my youthful years went.

Older people are treated with a great deal of respect and given the very best of everything while the youth do not get as much of an opportunity to prove themselves. One's youthful years are to be enjoyed, not something to be rushed through. This situation of wanting to get old as fast as possible depicts the irony of life. What makes more sense is for older people to wish they were younger and as physically fit as they once were. The reverse should not be happening. If you are young and reading this, don't wish all of your youthful years away. Enjoy your youth; you cannot stop time or speed it up. There is a time for everything. Certain things were not meant to be rushed; they will happen at their own pace.

There appears to be some confusion between being old and being mature or responsible. You don't have to be old in age to be considered as mature or responsible. Maturity and responsibility have more to do with the state of your mind than your age. Many people out there are old in age yet still behave like children; they are old, but have no sense of maturity and responsibility, which are things you develop. They do not automatically come to you just because of your age.

There are also people out there who think they are too old to be wrong. They believe that since they are so old, they have seen all there is to see and know all there is to know. For this reason, they believe they are always right. **But there is no such thing as being too old to be wrong.** Everyone is capable of making mistakes; there is always room to grow and learn more. At the same time, **there is no such thing as being too young to be right**. You can be young yet still knowledgeable.

The society has failed a lot of the youth who have been pushed over the edge so much that they feel they have no other choice but to join a life of crime just to make a living. While growing up in Nigeria, I can't remember coming across many kids who said that when they grew up, their sole life ambition was to become a scam artist, a pirate, a militant, an armed robber, or anything of that sort. Somewhere between when they are kids and when they become adults, they made certain life decisions based on their circumstances that steered them in the wrong direction. Society has a lot to do with why they choose this direction. Here is a scenario of how people turn out that way:

A young man graduates from high school (secondary school), but is unable to attend the already crowded universities. For that reason, he is forced to sit at home for years. He becomes desperate because he can't find a job and cannot gain admission anywhere. He looks to some friends who have resorted to illegal means to obtain money, appearing to be doing really well. They are driving fancy cars and wearing nice clothes. Deep inside of him, he doesn't want to do this, but it's getting increasingly difficult to survive. He is frustrated by his situation and he is desperate to make something of himself. He begins to think that his only option to make money is to do it illegally, just as his friends are doing. Before long, he summons up to the courage to move forward with it, and soon he is deep into a life of crime.

This young man did not have to end up this way. If he could have found better opportunities in life, chances are he would not have ended up the way he did. Also, if he had been surrounded with good examples of people to look up to, then good, upstanding people who made money through legal means could have shown him how he too could have done well for himself.

If you have ever felt tempted to go down the wrong path, know that you have better choices available to you. You do not have to go in the wrong direction to make money. Even when the opportunities around you are few, you can still make something great out of your life. Seek out the successful, upstanding people in your community. Find a way to connect so you can learn from them. Also, if you ever find yourself sitting at home for an extended period of time, doing nothing, get busy and engage yourself in meaningful work.

One of the most frustrating times in the youths' lives is when they are trying to find jobs. There are not enough open positions out there for the unemployed youth. When they find one, they are told they do not have enough working experience to get the job. It is frustrating: The youth cannot get a job because they do not have any experience, yet no one will give them a job so they can get the experience they need. It is a tough position for any person to be in and to figure a way out of. If you are in this position, know that perseverance is the key for you and in due time, you will find a job. Keep on pressing on and do not give up. Do not be shy or embarrassed about having to find a job—doing so will only hold you back from talking to certain people or seeking jobs in certain places. Be bold and talk to people about your situation. Look for opportunities to build work experience and go after them.

    If you are out looking for work and cannot immediately find one, do not get discouraged. Check newspaper advertisements and network with people who have access to the job you want. Another option is to volunteer your time with an employer for whom you'd like to work. Find out who makes the hiring decisions and let the person know that you are willing to work for free to gain experience. Very few people will turn down someone that wants to work for free. If you are accepted, show up to work every day on time, prepared to work hard. Even though you are working for free, work hard like you are getting paid to do it. Keep in mind that your goal while you are there is to impress the decision makers enough so they offer you a paying job. Prove yourself by becoming the best worker. You never know what might happen. A current employee might decide to leave, thereby opening up a position for you to fill. The company might even decide to expand and thereby hire you as an additional employee to fulfill their expansion needs. At the end of the day, when your volunteer time is over, even if they do not hire you, at least you now have the experience you need to get another job. The lack of job experience that you once had will no longer be a problem.

    When the mind is not engaged in something meaningful, it looks for something else to keep it occupied. This is one of the ways in which the youth get tempted to participate in crimes such as piracy, militancy, robbery, and fraud. If you don't feed your mind with positive things to keep it busy, it will seek out other things to keep it occupied.

Unfortunately, what your mind comes up with could be something negative and less than what you desire. Pay attention to this; don't end up where you don't want to be.

As members of society, we owe it to the youth to help them from losing belief. We also owe it to the ones who have already lost their belief to help them restore it. As long as they are still alive and kicking, there is hope for a better future for them. The youth should not be left to suffer and wander around in vain. Let's give them a helping hand. For those who want to help the youth, it can be overwhelming to decide whom to help. But start by picking one, two, or three people to work with and then do your best to guide and develop them. As you do so, instill in them the value of helping others so they can help others when they are in the position to do so.

The youth must get good exposure as early as they can in their lives. They are better able, then, to make good decisions about their future. It helps them discover their possibilities, the things they like, and the things they are passionate about. Having the right kind of exposure allows them to explore different professions that allow them to narrow down their desired profession. It also helps them understand what gets them motivated, what their natural talents are, and their strengths and weaknesses. When they discover these things, the youth are able to direct their efforts early and quickly toward the different areas of their lives where they have maximum impact.

We must praise and celebrate the things that the youth do well. It's easy to talk about their inadequacies or the things they do wrong. But if criticism is not delivered in a constructive way, it has a tendency to drag people further down. We have to reinforce their good behavior so they can continue to do more of it. We have to learn to give them encouragement when we can. We have to let them know when they are going in the right direction.

The women and the youth need to be given the opportunities they deserve to fully explore their potential instead of just being brushed off to the side. An increase in training opportunities must be established to help them grow as people and become self-sufficient. They need access to the right media to help them develop skills they need to prepare for employment.

Women and the youth are also encouraged to become innovative and pursue their own entrepreneurial ventures. The opportunities for women and the youth out there are boundless. There are industries dedicated to serving the needs of women and the youth that are yet to be fully developed. The women and the youth have a huge role to play in developing these industries. Since the markets for those opportunities already exist, they need to work among themselves to develop these opportunities together. As a part of the community of women and the youth, they have a lot in common with each other; they know each other's wants, needs, and desires. They must learn to take advantage of this level of mutual understanding, which will make it easier to work together.

As an entrepreneur, you have the opportunity to become a job creator instead of a job seeker. It puts you in a position not only to create job opportunities for yourself, but also to create employment opportunities for others. To get some useful tips about being an entrepreneur, study the chapter on entrepreneurship carefully—it will guide you on developing and growing a business.

Africa is currently regarded as having the greatest percentage of young people of any continent in the world. There are a lot of young people coming up that we cannot let down. If the youth are abandoned and left to become unproductive, society will only be worse off for it. All the potential lying within the youth cannot go to waste. Women and the youth are all needed for the work that lies ahead. We cannot afford to leave any talent, any dream, any skill or any potential behind. All of the resources available to us have to be used for the good of Africa. As we all work together, we can develop the continent to the level at which it should operate.

CHAPTER 10: DAILY AFFIRMATIONS

Daily affirmations are a mainstay in my life. They are empowering words I use every day to profess things into my life. I use affirmations this way based on my belief in the power of words. Affirmations are a decision to feel a certain way or to be a certain type of person. They can also be used to create specific results in your life by thinking and dwelling on certain thoughts. Affirmations could be a decision to feel empowered instead of powerless, to feel happy instead of sad, or to feel like a victor instead of a victim. Affirmations can be used to empower yourself to achieve the results you want and to create the life you want.

When using affirmations, you must be very clear about the results you want and very specific about your desired goal. Even if you aren't clear about how you'll achieve it, I want you to still profess the words. Your mind, as powerful as it is, will come up with ways to achieve your desired goal. If there is a certain area of your life in which you would like to be empowered, clearly articulate what you want in your affirmation. If, for example, you fear speaking in public, then your affirmation will be something like, "I am well prepared to give this speech" or "the crowd is going to love what I have to say." These affirmations will inspire confidence in you and enable you to deliver a better speech. As you continue to declare the affirmations, your mind will come up with ways to make what you are saying a reality.

Affirmations are a powerful tool; they can be used to create something new, as in the example above, or they could be used to eliminate something old from your life. Let's say you've made some wrong decisions and you would like to fix these problems. In your affirmation, you'll say something like, "From this day forward, I think thoroughly before making my decisions." Saying this regularly will imbed this thought into your mind and spirit so you will be constantly reminded to think thoroughly the next time you make a decision. By repeating this over and over again, it eventually becomes a part of who you are, so much so, in fact, that you'll rid yourself of the problem of making bad decisions.

When you say your affirmations, say them with full belief and without any doubt in your mind. Deep down you have to believe what you are saying. As you say the words, match your words with your body language, gestures, and your state of mind. Your whole body must be in sync with what you are saying so everything feels natural. When your entire being is in sync with your affirmations and you have no doubts whatsoever about what you're saying, your mind will develop complete belief, too. When your mind believes what you are saying, it then activates everything needed inside of you to make your affirmations happen.

With affirmations, repetition is very important. You do not just say the words one day and then never say it again for months; rather, you repeat these affirmations daily and as many times as you can per day. I recommend repeating them in the mornings, during the day, and then again in the evening. Through repetition, you can implant the words into your subconscious mind so they become part of you. It allows your mind easy access to the words and to draw on them when needed.

Say your affirmations out loud when you can. As you do, picture yourself living out the words of your affirmation by using the power of your imagination. Forming this mental image of yourself strengthens your affirmations, making them more achievable. As you also visualize doing what you are saying, your words become more believable and realistic. The more believable they become, the easier it is for you to make them happen.

In the same way that you can use words to positively affect your life, it is also possible to use words to negatively affect it. People negatively use words every day to impact their lives without knowing they are doing so. When they say things like "I am too old," "My body is weak," or "I can never be strong again," their mind picks up these things and tells their body to be that way. The more they say these negative things, the more their bodies respond to them. Over the years, I have met a lot of people who, through the use of continuous negative talk about their age, have begun to act much older than they really are. I see people who are forty-five acting like they are seventy-five through their own doing. If a fifteen-year-old child looks at himself in the mirror every day and says, "I am very old," over and over again, before long, he will feel old; his body will respond to what his brain tells him. For this reason, pay attention to the words you use and use words that only positively affect your life.

Learn to use your words wisely. If you fall into the category of people who use their own words to negatively impact their lives, put a stop to that. **Take charge of the words you use and take charge of your life.** Start replacing the negative words you have always used with positive ones so you can reverse the damage now. **Make a habit of talking about the things that you actually want in your life.** Speak them out loud so you can start attracting them into your life. Be careful about the names you call and what words you use when talking to others. Practice the golden rule: Treat others the way you would like to be treated; talk to others in the same way you would like them to talk to you.

Below are some examples of daily affirmations you can use to empower yourself. They are designed to empower different groups of people. There is a general affirmation entitled "Daily Affirmation" that can be used by anyone; there is an affirmation for women; an affirmation for the youth; and an affirmation for older members of society. Feel free to personalize the affirmations by adding or removing words as it suits you. Remember to repeat the affirmations as often as you can and to say the affirmations with complete belief and meaning. The more feeling you are able to combine with what you are saying, the more effective the words will be.

Daily Affirmation

Today is a new day and it brings with it a new set of opportunities for me to act on.
I am attentive to the opportunities and I seize them as they arise.
I have full confidence in myself and my abilities.
I can do all things that I commit myself to.
No obstacle is too big or too difficult for me to handle because what lies inside me is greater than what lies ahead of me.
I am committed to improving myself and I am getting better daily.

I am not held back by regret or mistakes from the past.
I am moving forward daily.
Absolutely nothing is impossible for me.

Affirmation for Women
I am a strong and powerful woman.
I am proud to be a woman and I celebrate the qualities that I have as a woman.
I am not defined by other people's opinion of who I should be or what I should do as a woman. I determine that, not anyone else.
I am not passed up for a position, title, or promotion because I am a woman.
I fully deserve all the good things that comes my way.
Irrespective of what anyone might think, being a woman places no boundaries or limits on my abilities.
I can do anything I set my mind to.
I celebrate my womanhood and I am beautiful both inside and out.

Affirmation for the Youth
I am fully capable of carrying out any job or task I am given.
I am not passed up for a position, title, or promotion because of my age.
I learn and acquire whatever skill or knowledge required of me to be successful.
I refuse to be held back from moving forward in life because of my age.
I acquire wisdom and valuable experiences that make me a better person.
I develop and practice good habits today that serve me well into the future.
My age is not an obstacle for me.

Affirmation for Older Members of Society
I have a sound mind and I am mentally alert.
I have good health and take good care of myself.
I am fully committed to making good, healthy choices.
I am open to change and capable of learning new things.
I am continuously growing and developing as a person.

My age allows me the opportunity to accumulate many wonderful life experiences, experiences that I use for my good and the good of others.
I share my knowledge and experience with others to help make them better.
I give and do a lot to make the world a better place.

Remember to repeat the affirmations daily. Use those that sound convincing and personal to you. Repeat them with full conviction and meaning. You are encoding them into your subconscious when you repeat them so they become a part of who you are. Say the affirmations in a bold, positive, and excited way. Be enthusiastic about each word you say. When you do this, the words will take power and will impact your life on a daily basis. They will raise feelings, powers, and abilities that lie dormant in you.

LESSON III: ACTION

Action is the fundamental key to all success.
—Pablo Picasso

To achieve any goal you set for yourself, you must take action. You will not achieve the dreams and desires that you have without taking action. Success is all about activity—it is about doing. Always take the steps you need to get you closer to where you want to be. The process of taking action begins with the thoughts in your mind. These lead to decisions, decisions lead to actions, and actions lead to results. So, first we think of something, then we make an internal decision about whether or not we want to act on that thought. Once we decide to take action, we then do so and our action brings about our desired results. Below is a visual depiction of what the sequence looks like:

Thoughts→Decisions→Actions→Results

Every chair, car, book, plastic, pen, phone, bag, and cloth that you see around you all began as a thought. Eventually, through an action or a series of actions, it became what you now see. In essence, what you see is just the result of that action, the end product of a thought. By understanding the pathway for getting results, we can make some very important deductions.

For you to get the right type of results, you must first think the right type of thoughts. Good actions, such as helping people in need, being honest, and being truthful, all start off with good thoughts. Bad actions, such as stealing, lying, cheating, and committing fraud, in the same way begin with bad thoughts. It is therefore important to guard your thoughts at all times. Take care in what you feed your mind and the kind of thoughts on which you dwell. If you dwell on negative thoughts long enough, they will manifest themselves as negative actions in your life. The same thing happens when your mind dwells on positive thoughts. Positive thoughts turn into positive actions, which further yields positive results. If you are thinking negative thoughts, always remember that a thought can be substituted with another thought. You can substitute a bad thought with a good thought, so you can ultimately have a good result instead of a bad one.

In the business world, it is important to note that people get paid for their actions and the results they get, not for their thoughts. Even though it all begins with thoughts, it is not what people focus on. This is another reason why it is important to take action. **You do not get paid for what you know, but for what you do with what you know and for what you are able to get others to do.** A doctor, for example, does not get paid a lot of money because of what he knows but because of what he does with what he knows. If you have great ideas, they will only remain ideas until you act on them. If you are at work, having valuable information in your head does no one any good until you put it to use or take action with it. Knowing is not the end product—it is only the beginning.

If you have a creative idea that can bring about change, you need to take action with it instead of just sitting on it. A light source put under the bed and covered up does not illuminate a room like a light source put out in the open to shine. Let your ideas shine by taking the appropriate action instead of keeping them in your head. Go ahead and shine; be the light in the world you were meant to be. You will be amazed at the effect your idea could have on people around the world. You are reading this book right now because of an idea that I had. Instead of sitting on the knowledge I had, I decided to take action by writing this book and sharing it with you. It is my hope that the ideas shared with you can bring about change in your life and help you become a better person. Remember, though: The ideas and knowledge you receive from this book can only make you a better person if you take action.

When you take the necessary action and get the results you hoped for, it inspires you to take more action again and again. By doing this, you can build momentum, and before you know it, you are achieving all the goals that you set for yourself. **Always remember that small wins add up to big wins.** Similarly, a collection of small results add up to a very big result. All the so-called "little successes" that you have form one big success when you put them all together. The momentum you generate from the little successes all work to your advantage and help you build consistency. As a result of the consistency you build from them, each individual result spurs you on to keep going for more results.

Results always accompany the action you take. But there are also results when you don't take action. For example, let's say you are faced with a situation where you have to take action in order to succeed. If you follow through by taking action, you succeed. If you do not take action, you fail. In both situations, success and failure are both results. There are consequences for whatever decision you make. It is up to you decide kind of result you want and to take the action that corresponds to that result.

Actions also alter the path of your life. You are where you are today because of the series of actions and decisions you made in the past. It is clearly logical, then, that if you want a better future, you can start taking the right actions today to shape your future. You can certainly build the future you want, but you must first start by identifying what you want and then taking the right action toward it. So, for example, if you want to get better grades in school, you must take the right action today by studying more. If you want to become a great athlete, you must take the right action today by training hard. Your future begins today. Start taking action toward the results you want today; if you successfully take the right action, you will successfully get the future you want.

If you know what you want, think the right thoughts concerning those results. Follow those thoughts with decisions that get you closer to those results. Finally, take action based on your decisions and you will start to notice results. Make sure you maintain the right level of activity when taking action by doing the most that you can do all the time. Since everything begins with thoughts, watch the thoughts that you think because, one day, they may become results.

If you ever get to the point where you find yourself just sitting around, wondering where you could be in life, get up and take action toward the life you want. Actions are what make the difference—not just thoughts, not just plans, but *actions*. You can spend all the time you want making plans, but until you take action, nothing changes. The same thing goes with intentions. Having the right intention is not enough; you must follow up your intention with action.

CHAPTER 11: FEAR AND OTHER OBSTACLES TO SUCCESS

Whenever I am in a difficult situation where there seems to be no way out, I think about all the times I have been in such situations and say to myself, "I did it before, so I can do it again."

Fear is one of the biggest reasons people do not take action. It has a paralyzing effect; it's a manifestation of different limiting thoughts that we plant in our minds. Fear tells us that we cannot achieve a goal, or that a situation is too difficult. These thoughts are designed to hold us back from taking action, but you cannot afford to be held back. Don't let it stop you from taking action and attempt to reach your goals.

Fear is a natural human tendency at play in different areas of our lives, even in the business world. The stock market, for example, reacts to just the thought of fear—when investors and traders are fearful that something bad might happen, it reflects in the stock market. This causes widespread panic and sell-offs, which often result in the market's decline. Even if the thing everyone fears never happens, the stock market is still affected.

Many times, the thought of fear itself is greater than what it is we fear. Our mind can make the very thing that we fear much larger and bigger than it really is due to the power of our imagination, which is able to intensify things, including fear. When this happens, the fear becomes so strong that it keeps you from what you need to do to succeed. Learn to see fear for what it is; don't blow it up and don't let it stop you from taking action.

Have you ever feared something so much that it ended up not happening? A lot of times, the things we fear will never happen. Yet your body and emotions still go through the process as if the very thing that you feared actually happened: You get headaches, emotional lows, and frustration. But you just went through all of this for nothing. Avoid putting such unnecessary stress on yourself.

I cannot guarantee that you will succeed every time you make an attempt at your goal, but I can guarantee that

you will fail every single time you do not make an attempt at your goal. For example, if you want to start a business but you do not take the time to register the business appropriately, learn about the demands of the business, and acquire the necessary skills and materials you need to start, then you cannot expect the business to magically run itself. Another example is if you have an exam to take but you do not take the time to prepare for it, pay attention in class, learn the book material, or even show up to take the exam. How can you expect to do exceptionally well on the exam? In cases like these, you will not achieve your goal unless you take action toward the things you need to do to succeed.

Fear can cloud your judgment by distorting your focus and making you less stable than usual. It also negatively affects your decision-making process. When taking action in fear, you are prone to making more mistakes as a result of your inability to focus. Whenever you notice fear holding you back, you must overcome it. You cannot let fear get in the way of your success.

To rid yourself of fear, focus more on what you are trying to accomplish than the fear itself. When you do this, what you try to accomplish becomes larger and more dominant in your mind than fear. As this happens, you become more committed to taking action toward your goal.

To move forward, you must discover what's holding you back. Sometimes, the best way to get rid of fear is confronting it. You must ask yourself: "What can I do to overcome this fear?" If some fears you have are made up in your mind, then you also have the ability to get rid of that fear. Empower yourself to overcome fear by using the power of your mind.

Lots of people have great ideas and plans for their lives, but they never take action and put it into motion. An idea will simply remain an idea until it is put to use. Below are some other reasons why people refrain from making their ideas into realities. These are things that eventually become obstacles to their success:

Dream Killers

These are individuals who you share your ideas with, but instead of encouraging you in a positive way, they laugh at you, telling you that your idea is no good and it won't work. But sometimes, they cannot see the big picture like you do or they are too scared to try what you are willing to try. When they see someone like you going for it, they try to discourage you. Be careful with such people; be wary of what you share with them. You don't need their approval of your idea or dream before you go for it. When I told people I was going to write this book, they laughed at me. They often questioned my decision to write it and laughed time and time again, but I did not let them kill my dream. I had a vision and I was sticking to it, no matter what: to help people achieve their life goals and help them become successful. Now that the book has been written and published, who is laughing now? Don't give the dream killers a chance.

Regret

Dwelling on regret can be limiting and disempowering. Let go of the past so you can grow. If you find yourself struggling with regret, seek the appropriate forgiveness from whomever you need and move on with your life. This gives you the freedom to move on with other matters in your life. Whatever happened in your past has already happened and cannot be changed. The only things that you can change are the things that have not happened yet. It is therefore important that you put your energy and focus in the right place. Focus on today and the things that are yet to happen. If you focus too much on something you did wrong in the past, you might miss important opportunities in the present. You only have twenty-four hours in a day; every time you worry about the past, you are wasting time that you could have been using to shape your future. Make a decision to spend your time wisely.

Procrastination

As much as people fail to admit it, procrastination is a form of laziness. It involves putting off things for a later time that actually should be done right away. We tend to make up excuses for why we cannot do what needs to be done right away: "I will get to it later," "I am too tired," or "I cannot do this right now." But all you are doing is lying to yourself. As a result of this, we usually wait till the very last minute to get things done, or we end up not doing them at all. The problem with doing things at the very last minute is that the quality of the work drops due to the time pressure faced. If you take the time to do something well the first time, you will probably do a better job at it. Also, in many cases, doing something the first time is less expensive than waiting till the last minute to do it. People think that if they wait long enough, the thing they are supposed to do will eventually disappear and they won't have to do it. The sad news for them is that it won't disappear.

To avoid procrastination, list the reasons why you need to do something. The bigger and more important those reasons are, the greater the chance that you will decide to follow through with what needs to be done. These reasons are a reminder to you of why it needs to get done. In addition, you can also make a list of what you stand to lose if you procrastinate. Being able to see the cost of procrastinating can encourage you to take action. Another way to avoid procrastinating is by breaking large tasks into smaller tasks. Since the smaller tasks look less daunting, you are more likely to take action.

Jealousy and Envy

Jealousy and envy have similar meanings: Jealousy is resentment toward someone for having something you believe should be rightfully yours, while envy involves the feeling of wanting something someone else has. They are both strong emotions that can cause extremely negative actions against other people. Both cases involve comparing one's life to others' and then feeling resentful toward them because they have something you do not have or that you fear losing. These things could include a job, position, trait, achievement, money, physical possession, or status. But in reality, there is no reason to be jealous or envious of anyone else, for you do not know how hard they had to work to achieve their success.

Stay clear of people who feel this way about you. Their negative feelings are designed to impede you from taking necessary actions toward your goals. This also helps you avoid the distractions that come with associating with people like this. All the distractions do is prevent you from achieving your goals. Avoid feeling jealousy and envy toward others. You have the ability to get the things you want if you are willing to take the necessary steps to get them. No need to worry about what other people have; focus on you and make things happen for yourself.

Rumor Peddling

This has been around for a long time. People talk a lot, so it's pretty common to hear what people say about you behind your back that are not necessarily true. It is easy for people to make up stories because they are jealous of you and what you are doing. They resort to smearing your name to slow you down. But you must focus on your goals; engage with them so much that you don't even have time to notice distractions or what is being said about you. If some of what is said does make it to you, **remember that you cannot always decide what people say about you, but you can decide how you choose to react to what they say about you**.

That's right: You have a choice in how you react and feel about what people say about you. When you hear what someone might say about you, you can choose to be sad, happy, or to completely ignore it. Make sure you make the right choice. Choose to remain happy, choose to remain focused on your goal, and choose to not be distracted off the path to success. Also, make sure you are not spreading rumors about other people. If you do not like people doing it to you, then you should not be doing it to others.

With rumors, you find that too many times people form opinions about other people without adequate confirmation from the person involved. For example, if there is a family member you do not hear from as often as you would like, it is easy to form the opinion that you are not hearing from the person because he or she doesn't care about you and the rest of the family. In reality, that person could be incredibly busy and engaged at work trying to keep a job, for example. It could also be because he or she has something else going on at this particular stage of life that needs his or her full attention.

Even if your opinions are based on certain things that have happened, they are still opinions and not fact. The moment we tell someone else these opinions, we give them life. Then that individual tells someone else, passing it off as a fact without mentioning that it started off as an opinion. Before you know it, you have a rumor spreading. Don't make up stories about other people. If you go around passing out made-up stories, you too have become a rumor peddler, which is not something you want to be.

Superstitions

Superstitions have been around since the beginning of time. In many cases, they begin out of fear or are designed to invoke fear in others. The basis of the fear is to prevent people from doing things that they would do otherwise if they were not in fear of it. With superstitions, people end up giving life to things that in reality have no life. Through their thinking, beliefs, or words, they give meaning to things that ordinarily have no meaning. But with superstitions, you have to keep an open mind. Do not necessarily agree or go with what other people say. When they speak to you out of fear or the beliefs that they have in their own minds, they try to convince you so you can also give meaning to things that have no meaning. Avoid following blindly. Also, seek wisdom, which allows you to see things as they really are and not how someone else tells you it should be.

Waiting for the Perfect Time

Sometimes, when you need to take action, you tell yourself to wait a little bit more or that it is not the perfect time to act. When you do this, time passes away, and before you know it, the opportunity is completely gone. Your decision to wait for the perfect time cost you an opportunity. But you just need to act right away; if you don't, the perfect time might never come. If you sit on an opportunity for too long, you just might lose it. Sometimes, your lack of decisiveness may lose you opportunities as well. But the perfect time is *now*.

Negative Self-Talk

Negative self-talk is a way of talking yourself out of success. You can tell yourself things like, "It is not possible," "I cannot do this," or "This is too difficult for me." But this will make you feel weak or incapable of doing something. This kind of talk ultimately stops you from taking action and doing what you need to do. The trick for overcoming negative self-talk is to reverse it and turn it into positive self-talk. When you do that, using the examples above, the self-talk becomes "This is possible," "I can do this," and "This is not difficult for me." Talking to yourself using positive self-talk empowers you to take action.

Lots of obstacles will come your way in life, but you must be steadfast with your goal to succeed. Obstacles are a part of life, and learning how to deal with them when they arise will serve you well in moving on with your goals. In going through these obstacles, you can discover things about yourself that you probably wouldn't have if you hadn't dealt with them.

Obstacles can also bring you opportunities. The problem, though, is that most people don't see the opportunities that come along because they are too focused on the obstacles. Learn to see this; by looking beyond the obstacles, you will see the opportunities behind them. Doing this gives you the fuel you need to keep going. There will be moments when you confront these obstacles that you will doubt yourself and ask, "Can I really do this?" Everything will make you feel like you can't, but always remember that you can.

Your desire to succeed must be stronger than the obstacle in your way. Remember this: **At the end, someone or something always gives up. It is either you give up and quit or the obstacle or failure gives up and makes way for your success to come through**. Don't be the one that gives up; leave that to the obstacle. Success is right around the corner for you. Just when everything feels overwhelming or too much to bear, you might be moments away from your breakthrough. Hang in there and be strong.

CHAPTER 12: HOW STRONG IS YOUR "WHY"?

If I asked you what you wanted in life, I am sure it would only take a few seconds for you to give me a quick list. They could be things such as money, a good job, a house, a new car, happiness, peace of mind, joy, and so on. All those things that you want are considered your WHAT. If I asked you a different question by asking the reason why you want those things, it would probably take you a bit longer to respond. Some people want money so they can buy things, a good job so they can earn lots of money, a house that is better than where they currently live, a new car to show off to their friends, or happiness away from their current misery. Whatever the reason that you want what you want, your reason is your WHY.

The WHY behind the WHAT is important for you to know because the WHY justifies the WHAT, serving as the reason for going after what you want. Everyone has a WHY behind what they do and what they want. The WHY varies from person to person, depending on the WHAT at any given time. Your WHY behind wanting a new car could be completely different from the WHY behind wanting a house. It could be to fulfill a desire or it could be out of need. Your WHY at any given time also varies in strength and importance. A weak WHY is of minimal meaning to you; a strong WHY, on the other hand, has a deeper sense of meaning. The stronger your WHY, the greater the reaction you'll have to it and the more likely it will cause you to take action.

A strong WHY is usually something of great significance, something of high importance that serves as a great source of motivation for you. When it comes to inspiring yourself, your WHY represents that something inside of you that spurs you on to take action. Whenever you think of it, it makes you want to start taking steps toward the things you want right away. It is the reason why you want to succeed. Your WHY drives you to get up every day to work toward your goals. It motivates you and gets you excited whenever you think of it; the mere thought of it stirs deep feelings inside you.

Your WHY could result from experiences you had while growing up; it could be a promise to provide your children with a good life, a personal commitment you made to never go back to a bad condition, a promise never to let your family suffer, or to glorify the God you serve. Regardless of what your WHY is, it serves the same purpose: It is the reason why you want to succeed.

Your WHY has to be personal. It has to be something that you came up with after a thorough examination of your life. It cannot be someone else's WHY or something you overheard somewhere that sounded really good. It is possible to share the same WHY as someone else, but it can't be just because you picked it up from that person. There must be a true connection between you and your WHY. This is what makes it mean so much to you and it is also why it pushes you to get your desired results.

Your WHY also has to be worthy of your success; it must be worthy of the time and resources you use to get your results. This is what sets apart a weak WHY from a strong WHY. If it is not worthy of your success, it will not drive you. You can't justify putting a lot of effort into something with a weak WHY. Your WHY should always urge you to take action. It should push you to go after your goals with everything you have. If your WHY doesn't do these things, then it's not serving a real purpose.

If you have yet to clearly define the WHY behind what you do, then you need to work on it. Clearly defining your WHY motivates you to reach your goals by helping you fully understand the reason behind what you do. A thorough introspection of your life will help reveal your WHY. No one else can come up with it for you—it must come from *you*. Everyone has different reasons for going after the results they want, so it's important that you discover your own reasons. This will also help you stay focused and committed to what you are doing.

To identify your WHY, think of what drives you. What fuels your passion? What makes you pursue goals in life? What moves you on the inside and gets you all fired up? Why do you get up every morning to go after your dreams? The answer to these questions is your WHY. Do you agree with the WHY you discovered? Make sure this WHY represents you. Does it fully embody who you are? It is important that you are in agreement with your WHY because it requires your total commitment. You must embrace it as your own for it to motivate you as much as it should. This will also help you stay committed to it.

Once you've identified your WHY and are in agreement with it, write it down and put it somewhere visible, such as in your room, shower area, where you dress, etcetera. Seeing it regularly allows it to serve as a constant reminder of why you do what you do. If you're worried someone else will see it, simply writing down the words "Remember WHY" will do as well.

You could also use a photo or some other thing to represent your WHY. I also recommend looking at your WHY in the mornings before you start your day. It will remind you of why you are getting up in the morning, why you are going to work, why you work so hard, and why you do what you do. When you look at your WHY, even on the worst days when you're not feeling energetic, you will feel an immediate burst of energy and you will be ready to go. That is how powerful your WHY can be.

Some people discover what their WHY is, but somewhere along the way, they forget about it. They get caught up in the daily routine of life and completely lose the meaning behind their actions as well as losing focus and straying from their original intentions. They simply forget the reason why they were on their road to success. This is why it's important to keep your WHY in front of you—so you don't forget. You can also share your WHY with close friends and family members to remember it, people whom you trust will use the knowledge of your WHY for good. In case you ever forget it or you stop thinking about it, they will remind you. When you are feeling down or uninspired, these individuals can help motivate you by recalling your WHY and get you back on course.

When tough times come, a lot of people tend to fold up and quit. Their desire to press on simply fades away. If you have a strong WHY, however, you can easily get through these tough times because it will motivate you to keep going, regardless of obstacles. With a strong WHY, things will no longer feel out of reach for you. You will have the extra boost you need to go on so your situation doesn't stop you from going after what you want.

A strong WHY could also prevent you from making bad choices. When you think of your WHY and the consequences of making a bad choice, it makes you rethink your actions. Since your WHY is important to you and you don't want to jeopardize it, you will make good choices for yourself.

A strong WHY can also overpower your weaknesses, something that most people are insecure about. They try to cover up their weaknesses so people don't notice them. They also stay away from doing anything that involves operating in an area where they are weak. When you have a strong WHY, even your weaknesses do not stand in your way. The first thought that comes to your mind is not about your weakness, but is instead about your WHY. If there is something you need to do, you'll do it because your WHY is more important than any weakness.

There are no limits for you when operating with a strong WHY. Ordinarily, you might rethink your actions or stop when you get to a certain point, but that doesn't happen with a strong WHY. It makes you push through and past any potential limits you may encounter. Even past failures won't stop you. In cases where you previously failed at something because of a weak WHY, you won't be afraid to try it again because your reason for wanting to succeed is different.

Having a strong WHY also gives you an edge over your competitors because you have a stronger desire to succeed. Where your competitors may lack motivation or only have weak WHYs, you will be more motivated. Your strong WHY makes you want it much more, which is reflected in your attitude and your actions toward what you are doing. Your competitors may be limited in how far that they can go, but you are willing to push all the way.

Your WHY creates a sense of urgency in you. In many situations, you may be slow to take action, taking your time because there is no real reason for you to be in any hurry. But when you have a strong WHY, this is not the case. When you think of your WHY, your attitude goes from "I will do something about it later" to "I am going to do something now." Since your WHY is very important to you, you cannot afford to let it fall by the wayside. You treat it with urgency so it gets the attention it requires.

Find out what your WHY is and clearly define it. Once you do, put it where it will serve as a constant reminder, a place where every time you see it, it will motivate you to do the things you need to do. We need a strong reason to do some things in life. If we don't have one, there will be no energy and things won't get done. And sometimes we need to make changes in our lives, but to do so, we require a strong desire and motivation. And still there are times when life knocks us down and we need a reason to get back up. These are all times when we need a strong WHY. It will help you get through your struggles, it will help you endure through pain, and it will give you the courage you need to continue.

CHAPTER 13: THE POWER OF FOCUS

Concentrate all your thoughts upon the work at hand. The sun's rays do not burn until brought to a focus.
—Alexander Graham Bell

I have always been full of ideas of all kinds. When it came to pursuing those ideas, I would try to do too much at once, and for that reason, nothing got done. I spread myself out in different directions and although I worked hard at these ideas, I didn't get the results I wanted. Then I learned about the power of focus. When I focused on one thing at a time instead of trying to do fifty things at once, my results dramatically improved.

It's easy to think that working hard automatically means you are getting things done. The truth is, those two things do not always equate to each other. In most cases, if you just increased your level of focus for a good amount of time, you wouldn't have to work as hard and your time would be spent more efficiently.

To put things into perspective, imagine you are chasing three rabbits at the same time. How many of those rabbits do you think you could catch? While chasing these three rabbits, you probably think you are working really hard. But the truth is, you may end up not catching any rabbits at all. This is especially so when all the rabbits are running in different directions. You are better off trying to catch one rabbit first, then moving onto the second rabbit, and then onto the third rabbit. This allows you to focus on one rabbit at a time, thereby giving you a greater chance of success.

The same thing applies to your daily work. **It is not so much about how many hours you spend on your work, but how many hours you spend focused on your work.** Spending time on your work and being focused on your work are two completely different things. Sometimes you might be physically at work, but your mind is elsewhere, daydreaming about unrelated things and therefore inefficiently performing your job. Being focused, on the other hand, allows you to be more efficient.

A lot of people start different things but never see them through, losing focus along the way. When you choose not to focus on one thing and see it through, you end up with a lot of unfinished things and eventually you become overwhelmed by them. Some people do this over and over again till it becomes a habit, bringing a lot of stress with it, not to mention the amount of energy, time, and money wasted on bouncing around between different things.

The ability to focus greatly increases your productivity. A higher level of productivity means can get more done within a specific amount of time. It makes you more valuable to your employer because you require a lot less company time to get things done. By being productive, you also save the company money by reducing the amount of employees that need to do the work that you are doing. You are more valuable to yourself because you can free up more time to do other things.

You can practice working on one thing at a time by learning how to prioritize. If you have a lot to do, put everything down on a list and rank each item according to how important it is. Put the most important thing as number one on your list, followed by the second most important thing, and so on until you get to the bottom of the list, which will be the least important thing. When it is time to start working on the listed items, start from the beginning and you work your way to the very bottom of the list.

Whatever you focus on grows. When driving and looking in a certain direction, you will slowly drift toward the direction in which you focus, as if you are being pulled in that direction. This also applies to your life and goals. Focus on where you want to go and your mind will move you in that direction. If you focus on success, you will see more of it; if you focus on failure, you will see more of it. Examine your life as it is right now: What are you paying the most attention to? Is it something that you truly want more of in your life? If it is not, then you need to shift your focus to what you really want more of. Only then can you begin to see more.

If what you focus on grows, be clear about it and why it is your focus so you don't attract the wrong things into your life. Think logically about your choices and make sure you make decisions to focus on the right things. By being clear about your focus, the process also makes clear the results you expect, which gives you direction.

What you focus on expands and we always get more of what we focus on. Most people make the mistake of focusing solely on their problems. When you do this, they will grow and expand. You must focus on the solutions to problems and not the problems themselves. When you focus on solutions, then that is what will expand in your life.

This applies to everything in your life. If you focus on getting better grades at school, then you will start getting better grades because you've put all your attention toward that goal. You are also more aware of the things on which you focus. For example, if you are wearing a red shirt and you focus your attention to the fact that you are wearing a red shirt, you will all of a sudden notice other people also wearing red shirts.

Staying focused is also an efficient way to control mistakes. Mistakes happen when you rush through things or you're not focused on what you're doing—you're more likely to miss things. But you are more likely to do things correctly when you focus.

Your focus plays a big role in how you feel. By changing what you focus on, you can change how you feel inside. For example, if you only focus on the things that are going poorly in your life, you may feel bad about yourself. If you instead focus on the things that *are* going well in your life, then you can feel positive about yourself, putting you in a much better mood.

There are so many things vying for your attention on a daily basis. These distractions can easily come from anywhere and at any time. The majority of distractions can be avoided through adequate preparation. Before starting something that requires your focus, effectively prepare for it by removing or avoiding any potential distractions. If you are still distracted, remove yourself from the situation by taking a break for a few minutes and refocus before continuing your task.

When I was at the university, I once played in a five-a-side soccer tournament, where a team of five players play against another team of five players. On this particular day, we had been scheduled to play another team in the knockout stage of the competition—the team that won the game continued on in the tournament while the other team would be kicked out. When the time came to play the game, two players on the other team didn't show up. So instead of playing five versus five, it ended up being five versus three. My team's players were excited. To us, it was an opportunity to beat them and move on in the tournament.

My team was made up of five Africans while the other team was made up of three non-Africans. Rather than forfeiting the game and getting automatically kicked out of the tournament, the other team decided to play. We had one player in goal with four outfield players while the other team had one player in goal and only two outfield players. Right before the game started, one of my African teammates said, "This is going to be an easy win for us; we are going to score a lot of goals."

Shortly after, the referee blew the whistle and the game started, and as embarrassing as it sounds, the other team beat us. Both of our teams had similar abilities and similar fitness levels, and yet they beat us. We were shamefully kicked out of the tournament.

That day I learned something very powerful about Africans. If you ever want to disrupt a group of Africans, plant a seed of confusion within them; let them lose focus on the task at hand, sit back, and watch them do the rest. They will argue, blame each other, trade blows, and fight among themselves till they self-destruct. This is exactly what happened to my team. The other team scored one goal on us by accident and that was all it took. Our team argued and blamed each other for the mistake, and nobody wanted to back down. Everything turned chaotic. One argument led to another and each time a player blamed another player, it only led to more blame going in the other direction. We beat our own selves that day.

Due to the arguments and infighting, we broke our concentration. We lost focus on what we were trying to achieve, which was winning the game. At the end of the game, we were exhausted. We had run more than we needed to run. We had shouted more than we needed to shout. I remember looking at the other players while panting with fatigue and thinking to myself, "I cannot believe we just lost this game." We were all so ashamed.

How many times do you see incidents like this happening? How many times do you see it in professional soccer teams, schools, business, families, and with our leaders? Such things happen all the time. People get distracted by a certain matter, argue and fight over it, and even go as far as starting a war. Through it all, they lose focus on their primary goal. We not only have to stay focused, but as a community we have to do better with conflict resolution. Not every difference in opinion has to lead to a fight.

You will come across many things designed to make you lose focus. Once you find somewhere or something that you want to focus your energy on, engage and immerse yourself in it with all your energy. Distractions will come in different shapes, sizes, and personalities, but no matter the distraction that comes your way, always maintain your focus. Your ability to do so will give you clarity and a calm mind. Don't lose sight of what you are trying to accomplish. Even your best friend or family member can be a distraction to you. Be sure about what you want to accomplish and commit your focus to it. No matter what bumps you run into, keep your focus on your destination. Keep going and heading in that direction and you will see dramatic results in your life.

CHAPTER 14: PLANNING AND GOAL SETTING

To dream of success is to set a goal of where you want to be; to wake up, take action, and achieve it is what true success is all about.

Planning and goal setting are two essential keys to success in life. Without them, you are basically roaming through life aimlessly. Imagine a boat out in the middle of the ocean with no anchor and no one controlling it. The boat will move in whatever direction that the power of the wind and the ocean pushes it to. This is what it's like to go through life without a plan or goals. If you do this, life will push you around in any direction that it wants to. You will lose control and the ability to steer yourself in the right direction. **You just can't let life happen to you, you have to make life happen.** Live your life with intention. Live your life with a direction in mind. Make plans for yourself and set goals according to what you want.

Goal setting and planning is about knowing where you are, where you want to go, and what you need to do to get there. If you don't know where you're going, how do you know how to get there? Even if you make it there somehow, how do you know you are where you want to be? You can only know these things if you know where you are going to begin with. You could be standing in the very position that you want to be and you wouldn't know it because you don't have the destination in mind. In the same way, if you don't know what you are looking for, then you will not know how and when you find it, even if it's something easily accessible. Creating a plan and a goal cannot be underestimated.

There is a reason why majority of the people with goals do better than those without—they know in which direction they are heading. People with goals also do better because they know what they want and have a plan to get it. You must have a plan in place to take action to attain the success you want. In this chapter, we will delve more into the process of creating a plan and setting goals on which you can act.

When setting and pursuing your goals, it's important to start with the WHAT. If you are clear about the WHAT, the

HOW will take care of itself. The WHAT are the goals that you want to achieve while the HOW is the way to go about achieving them. It is an important distinction to understand because too many people put one before the other. Set your goals first, and then work out the HOW from there. When you set your goals, everything else that you need will eventually come to you.

I will now go over what it takes to properly set goals. First, I will list the different steps for achieving your goals and then talk about each step in more detail. If you follow these steps carefully, they will guide you toward actualizing your goals. Below is the six-step process:

Step one: Evaluate yourself
Step two: Decide on your goals
Step three: Organize your goals
Step four: Strategize
Step five: Take action
Step six: Track your goals

Step One: Evaluate Yourself

Evaluating yourself is about taking an accurate assessment of exactly where you are relative to where you want to be. When going through the evaluation process, try to think clearly and objectively about yourself. Analyze your personal situation to see what you have done and what you are yet to do. Evaluating yourself is about going into the core of who you are. It is also about evaluating the habits you have. Look at which habits hold you back, which habits propel you forward, which habits you need to get rid of, which habits you need to keep, and which new habits you need to adapt. Be frank with yourself during this process for an accurate assessment.

Step Two: Decide on Your Goals

The next step is to design goals around where you want to be. Make these goals very specific, but don't create too many or make them confusing. When you are specific, you are giving your brain a particular set of instructions on where to focus. For that reason, your goals should be definite and straightforward, as well as your decisions.

Make your goals measurable—you should be able to tell at any given time how well you are doing in meeting your goals as well as when the goals have been met. Whether your goal is halfway completed or 100 percent completed, it should be easy to measure. Another important thing is to write your goals down. There is power in doing so. People tend to stay more committed to accomplishing goals when they are written down; being able to see them visually makes your goal more real. Writing down your goals in detail feeds your imagination. Your imagination in turn makes the goals more believable. Goals that are believable are achievable.

Set goals for yourself that are challenging, but realistic. The goals should stretch you, but within reason. The goals should not be set so high that they are not believable to you or that they discourage you from trying to achieve them. Your goals should also not be set so low that they are easily achievable with minimum effort on your part. Aim high enough with your goals so they fully engage you; aim high enough that they bring the best out of you to achieve them.

Step Three: Organize Your Goals

Organize your goals by their order of priority. The most urgent should be listed at the top, and the least urgent at the bottom. Each goal should have an anticipated completion date and time on it, which will create urgency toward pursuing your goals. The completion date should be close enough that it creates the right kind of pressure for you to get it done.

If you also have big goals that appear too difficult or impossible, break them up into small parts, which will make them appear less intimidating. Organize and sort the goals logically so when you get through all the small parts, it all adds up to your big goal.

Step Four: Strategize

The next step is to put together a strategy for how to achieve those goals. This is when you ask yourself: "What can I do every day to move me closer toward achieving my goal? How do I get from where I am to where I want to be? How do I need to behave to achieve my goals?"

When putting together a strategy, be realistic and specific about the things you need to do: the amount of time, money, support, and anything else you need that will be involved. You must also find out what you need to sacrifice to achieve your goals. It could be time that you spend sleeping, or even playing.

I recommend reviewing and reciting your goals daily to develop a mental commitment toward achieving your goals. As this commitment grows, your mind will develop a plan to achieve those goals. Soon enough, your life and your actions will conform toward achieving them, too. Technology can also be used to aid the process of reviewing your goals every day. Something as simple as a cellphone can be used to set reminders to review your goals. Depending on how sophisticated your cellphone is, you could even program your goals into your cellphone so they automatically pop up at a certain time every day to review them. This is something that I do.

Once you complete this step, create a plan to achieve your goals. This plan must delineate exactly what you need to do. Follow the best strategy to get things done.

Step Five: Take Action

This is a very important step. Your goals will require your full commitment and sustained effort. Without taking this step, nothing changes. You must now follow through with your plan and strategy. Do something whenever you can toward your goals. The more action you take, the greater the chance your goals will become a reality.

If you have trouble taking action, there are a few things you can do to inspire yourself. First, you can visualize achieving your goals. Take time to think about what achieving your goals means to you. How would your life change if your goals were achieved? How would things look? How would you feel? Don't forget to be specific. If you can visualize these things, the feeling and thought of them will be so strong that they will drive you to take action. This is also a good point to think of what your WHY is.

As you do more and begin to achieve your goals, the feeling of achievement will push you toward taking action toward your other goals, since success breeds more success. Success also builds up your self-esteem, which gives you the confidence to go after your goals.

Step Six: Track Your Goals

Finally, as you take action toward achieving your goals, it is important that you track and monitor them, regardless of the type of results you get or the stage you are at. Ask yourself: "Am I getting the results that I want to see?" Doing this allows you to know how well you are doing in meeting your goals. By keeping track of things, you can measure your results, efforts, and which goals you have met or those you have yet to meet. Tracking your goals also allows you to know when and where to make adjustments along the way. Review your goals regularly and make updates to them as you need to. A review lets you know whether or not you are heading in the right direction. In this step, you get to inspect what you expect to happen.

At times in my life, I would set up annual goals, but I wouldn't meet them at the end of the year. I almost got discouraged about not meeting the goals, but as time passed, the goals unceremoniously crept up, and I achieved them. What I later found was that the goals I had set for myself were planted in my subconscious mind as soon as I wrote them down. My subconscious mind pushed me toward achieving those goals, even though I was not fully aware of it. There is power in setting goals—the very act of setting goals helps set things in motion. Don't be discouraged if you don't meet a goal exactly when you want to. Keep taking action toward it, and eventually your goals will become reality. Sometimes, you may feel like you are not getting ahead, but things are already in motion for you to be achieved at a later date.

One of the biggest mistakes that people make when setting a goal is looking at their life as it is or what they have done in the past and then basing their ability to meet a goal at a future date solely on that. They say, "Look at my life. It is impossible for me to achieve this goal." They say this even though they don't know what the future holds for them.

You have to believe in yourself. If you are committed to meeting a goal and ready to do what it takes to meet it, then it is possible. **Do not let your past hold you back from what you think you can achieve in the future.** Whatever happened in the past is in the past; the future holds immense possibilities for you, provided you are willing to put in the effort required. **The person that you were in the past might not have been able to meet your goals, but you have everything in you to become the person you need to be now to meet those goals.**

Another common mistake is when people feel bad about the things they do not have yet or the goals they are yet to achieve. Don't ascribe negative feelings toward your goals—they are meant to inspire you, not make you feel bad or depressed. If you are in a bad emotional state, you are less likely to take action toward achieving your goals. If your goals inspire you, on the other hand, you feel energized about them and are more likely to push yourself toward achieving them. Be inspired; even though you have not achieved your goals yet, you are well on your way.

Finally, aim to be a goal achiever and not just a goal setter. The difference is in the results. Become a goal achiever by getting things done. Most people get excited when embarking on a new goal, but the excitement fades as they run into challenges or lose their motivation. This is very common with New Year's resolutions. At the beginning of the year, people talk about all the wonderful things they would like to do in the new year, but by the time it comes around, the majority of them quit on their goals. Some may pursue their goals for a few days or even a few months, but they don't hang on long enough to see them through the whole year. Learn to develop staying power to see your goals through to the end.

Your goals have a way of changing you for the better. To achieve certain goals, you must become a certain kind of person. Depending on the nature of your goals, you may have to become much more hardworking, attentive, efficient, and focus-driven. Set good goals for yourself and do not be afraid to pursue them. You start to become the person that you need to be to achieve those goals. In the long run, you will not only achieve your goals, but you will also become a better person.

CHAPTER 15: FOCUS ON THE PROCESS AND NOT THE RESULT

A lot of people talk to me about how much money they would like to make. They focus on money and all the things they can do with it. They talk about the cars they could buy, the beautiful homes they could have, and the other nice things they would buy if only they had the right amount of money. They think about money and worry about it all the time. I try to let them know that their focus is on the wrong thing. Make no mistake: **Making money is the result of a series of thoughts, decisions, and actions that are set into motion**. Focus on the process of making money, not just the result. The result is the last step. When you focus on the right thoughts, decisions, and actions, the result will come. If you have the right process in place and you are doing everything correctly, the money will come and you won't have to chase it. I always tell people to chase the process, not the money. The same thing goes with success in anything. The success you obtain is all about the effort you put into the thing you are doing. Success, happiness, good health, confidence, joy, a long life, a high paying job, and other things people want are all results. Take a good look at the result you want and focus on the process that will get you there. In other words, see the big picture and the end goal first, and then get busy on the process to make it happen. When you focus on the process and get it right, the result just automatically happens—even science backs this up. Newton's third law states that for every action there is an equal and opposite reaction. This means that for every action that you take, there is bound to be a reaction as a result of it. **The process is the action you take while the result is the reaction you get.** The process has more to do with the path you follow and the result is where you end up.

Here is a story of two friends that were after the same result but followed two different paths to obtain it. After reading the story, I want you to guess which of the two friends was more likely to reach that result. These friends both lived in Ghana but wanted to visit South Africa for the holidays. They didn't have the money they needed to travel, but they were determined to go on the trip. In order to this, they would both have to save up money in the months leading up to the trip. The first friend, whose name was John, thought about South Africa a lot. He could not get South Africa off his mind. He thought about the things he would do when he got there. He thought about Cape Town and Johannesburg and all the other cities he would like to visit when he got to South Africa. He also thought about the different landmarks and tourist attractions he would visit when he got there. He wondered about the weather there and how it was similar to or different from the weather in Ghana. He thought about the language in South Africa and how he would communicate when he got there. He wondered about the food and if it was prepared just the way he liked it.

The other friend, Peter, who also wanted to visit South Africa, did things a little differently. He started by researching the different airlines that flew into South Africa from Ghana. He found out how much the different airlines charged and the best time to book his flight. He also estimated how much he would spend when he got there. After calculating how much he needed for the entire trip, he came up with a savings plan to accumulate the requisite amount of money. He knew if he put away a certain amount of money every week, he would have all the money he needed by the time he was ready to travel. He stayed committed to his savings plan and did exactly what he was supposed to do. When it was time to go, he had all the money he needed in hand to travel to South Africa.

With all things being equal, which one of these two friends do you think ended up visiting South Africa for his holidays? If you guessed correctly, it was Peter. His preparation greatly improved his chances of traveling to South Africa. He was more focused on the process of getting everything he needed to travel than he was on the outcome or result of going to South Africa. John, on the other hand, focused more on South Africa and what he would do when he got there rather than what he needed to do to get there. The right approach for both friends was to keep the goal of traveling to South Africa in mind, but to focus more on how to get there.

If you don't know how to get to where you are going, how do you expect to get there? This in itself is a life principle. First determine where you want to go, then figure out how to get to where you are going and what you need to do to get there. Once you have these things figured out, getting to your destination becomes so much easier for you to achieve.

If you also focus more on money than you do on the process of making money, you are more likely to cheat, cut corners, commit fraud, or steal. When you constantly think of money all the time and you are not making the money you desire, it's easier for money to become an obsession. It then completely consumes your thoughts and makes you more likely to turn to any means necessary to obtain it. A lot of this comes out of desperation, but don't get to this point. If you do, seek appropriate help immediately before you do something that you will forever regret.

The wrong means of getting money don't offer long-term satisfaction; you end up paying for your actions in one way or another. Making money the right away is far more rewarding and enjoyable than making money the wrong way. When you make money the right way, you don't have to live your life in fear or constantly worry about the police showing up at your house. You don't have to worry about the day when people find out about what you did. Choose the right way, the way that offers long-term satisfaction and peace of mind.

You are more in control of what is happening now than you are of what is yet to happen. The result you are looking for is usually in the future, while the process is in the present. Knowing that what you do in the present affects what happens in the future enables you to make changes in the present as needed so you can have the future you hoped for. For example, if you want a high-paying job when you graduate from school and you know that good grades will help you achieve that goal, then you have to study hard and do well in school. **When you do the things in the present that you can see, you are shaping the future that you are yet to see.**

When you focus on the process, you learn more and become better at it. This allows you to better evaluate the steps that you need to go in the right direction. If your end goal is to have a high-paying job, you can learn more about which studying techniques work better for you by focusing on the process. You can find out if studying at night is better for you than studying during the day. You can learn more about how many hours you need to study every day until you fully understand the material. By focusing on the quality of your work, you can increase your chances of getting better grades. You can also focus on getting the right kind of training and experience that would be beneficial to you in landing the job you want.

The same is also true for an athlete. If you want to become better at running, playing football, or any other sport, you must focus more on practicing and training. The more you practice, the better you get. Practicing regularly also makes it easier for you to perform a particular skill. When you focus on these things in training, you can more easily execute what you have practiced during a game.

You must learn to love going through the process just as much as you love the result. The more you love it, the more you are willing to do, which will turn into getting more of a good result. If you do not love the process, it will be easy for you to quit. If you want to become a top athlete but you hate training, you probably won't train as often as you need to do. But since you are required to train hard to reach that goal, you won't achieve the result you want, which is to be a top athlete. Since training hard is the process that gets you the result you want, you must develop a love for it so you can get the result you want.

In the same vein, a business that focuses more on making money than on making quality products or offering good service to its customers will not make money to its full potential. By focusing only on money, the quality of your products will suffer; as a result of this, your customers will turn to your competition for the products they want, which will lead to the decline of your profits. On the other hand, focusing on making quality products and having great customer service helps attract more customers to your business. When your business successfully does this, it is then able to make more money.

The quality of the results you get in life is directly related to the quality of the effort you put into the process. Your life as it is today is an indication of the things you have done in the past up until this point. If you put a sub-par effort into the process, you will get a sub-par results. If you put an outstanding effort into the process, you will get outstanding results. In the same way, the habits you have in your life right now also greatly influence the results you see. Your habits determine how you work through the process. Having lazy habits means that you work through the process in a lazy way and will affect your results negatively. By developing new positive habits, you can change the results you get in your life positively.

Getting the process done correctly is going to require your commitment and hard work. Understand that if you put your all into it, the process will reward you with the right results. Being lazy is not an option. Work is good to the person who does it; it makes you a better person. You should enjoy working, since it comes with its rewards. Your reputation as someone who works hard and gets things done attracts other people to you; they know they can rely on you and your level of influence starts to grow. Whether you are working hard or working smart, it is all part of the process.

What does it matter how much work you had to put into the process when you can step back and look at the wonderful result you get out of it? An artist who puts a lot of time into painting a magnificent piece doesn't bemoan how long it took to paint because he is proud of the finished product. The dividends you get from the result far outweigh the work you put into the process. Be willing to do the work. When the results come, it will be all worth it.

Thoughts to ponder about work
I have never been scared to work.
I believe work is my friend.
Having no work is what bothers me.
If I do not have any work, something less desirable might take its place.

Everyone sees the results, but not everyone sees the process. When you are successful and able to get the results that you hoped for, everyone can see the results and not the process. They do not see the long hours you had to work, your dedication to learning about what it takes to get the right kind of results, or how difficult things were for you. All they see is the result. Some may think that you were just lucky. Some may think that you don't deserve the result. Some may even think that someone else handed you the result. But what's most important is what *you* think and what *you* know. Remember, it's okay if no one knows how much you put into the process—at the end of the day, you got the result you wanted.

When you make up your mind to get a certain kind of result, it can look overwhelming at times, so much so that you get discouraged from pursuing it. That's why you must focus on the process by breaking it down into small steps that are manageable and do not overwhelm you. Next, work through the process one step at a time as best as you can, and eventually you'll have the result you want.

If you're not getting the results you want, recognize it as feedback. It might be from one step in the process or a number of steps. It might be that you're taking the wrong steps or that you're not executing the steps the way you should. Flaws in the process usually manifest themselves in the result. To fix it, review the steps that you took, and upon a thorough review, you should be able to spot the flaws in the process. With the necessary adjustments to your steps, you should begin to get the results you want.

There will be times that you feel like quitting the process. Things may become unbearable, and you'll become discouraged. But maintain your focus; don't let anything get to you. Lock yourself into the process. By applying the right amounts of effort, patience, persistence, and wisdom, you can overcome any trial you face. The process is your key to the results. **To get to your place of victory, intended destination, and the success you want, you must go through the process.** The trials you face are only a part of it. **If you quit on the process, you are quitting on the results.**

LESSON IV: LEADERSHIP

When most people think of leaders, they immediately think of the government: state government, federal government, and all other government officials in various capacities. The government's inadequacies and failures are also a common topic on the lips of many Africans. Even when you talk to government officials, like lawmakers, ministers, and governors, they themselves talk about how bad the government is as though they are not part of it. They refer to other government officials as bad and corrupt, which shows a lack of responsibility on their part.

While clearly the government doesn't do enough for its people, you must recognize that that you are a leader, too. You don't have to be in any specific position of authority or power to be a leader; you can lead from wherever you are in life. You can lead as a student, trader, driver, police officer, farmer, security officer, messenger, or wherever it is you find yourself. You can be a leader without serving in a government role.

Your life is your own responsibility—it's too important for you to put in the hands of someone else. You can no longer afford to sit around and wait for what the government might do for you. Take full control of your own life; take action so you can be the best you can be for yourself. When you do this, any help you get from the government along the way is a bonus. Taking ownership of your own life strengthens and empowers you to make a difference. Taking ownership of your life also gives you a different perspective on things, which allows you to see things more clearly. You can also identify what you need to do to get the results you want.

For those who are always complaining about how bad their leaders are, I understand your frustration but I want to challenge you to **be the leader that you want to see in your community**. You have been complaining for far too long, and nothing has changed. So do something about it. The change begins with *you*. I am not asking that you save the world in one day—just start wherever you are. Start in your community, school, village, family, workplace, start somewhere, anywhere. The work you do will spread and take root. When others see what you are doing, it will attract likeminded people to join in and support you.

If you look at anything successful, you will find traces of a good leader in it. It doesn't matter if it is a successful movie, sports team, school, business, family, or government, there will be an effective leader involved in it. Leadership isn't something that can be ignored. When good leadership is absent, everyone sees it and a lot of people are affected by it.

Most people believe that all leaders are born to lead. This is a big misconception because leaders are made, not born. You, too, can be a great leader; to do this, you must commit to learning what it takes to be a leader and what the great leaders before you did. Becoming a big student of learning in every way is important. You must read books about leadership and also study the ways of great leaders. Find out what makes them great leaders, why people like them became leaders, and how they go about their work.

You must first develop yourself before you lead others. It is always a good idea to learn something first before trying to teach others. You practice what you learn till it becomes a part of who you are. The more you work on yourself, the better leader you will become.

You must dig deep to find out the purpose of your leadership. You must find answers to questions about who you are, why you are in this position, and what you should be doing. This can be done by developing an understanding of your life story and finding out how it ties to the leadership position in which you find yourself. Look for the connections and find out what it all means. From there, determine exactly what you want your leadership to be about. What type of results are you looking for? Get a clear picture of it.

As a leader, your words are important. Words used correctly can move people to action and inspire them. **Sometimes, it is not about what you say, but how you say it.** Learn to use words for effect. Pausing at the right time or putting emphasis on certain words are just some of the ways you can completely change the way your message is received. Some of the greatest leaders have been known for their mastery of words. Their speeches are remembered in history for the powerful effect they had.

As a leader, your actions and the things you say will be closely monitored, so it's very important to do as you say you will do. Continuous talk with no substance to back it up will lead to followers questioning your leadership. They will wonder if you are really capable of doing the things you say and may slowly lose trust in you. Doing as you said you would, on the other hand, shows that you can be counted on. It lets people know that your word means something, conveying trust and building on your leadership. The great thing about keeping your word is that if you do it consistently, you'll never have to worry about breaking a promise again. It will become a part of who you are.

Leadership comes with great responsibility, something you must recognize from the very beginning. Recognizing this early on allows you to prepare mentally for the responsibility you are about to take on. If you lead a group of people directly, who in turn lead another group of people, then when something goes wrong your leadership can't be all about pointing fingers and blaming only those people whom you have led directly. You have to accept that, as a leader, you are partly responsible for the things that go wrong with the people you have led both directly and indirectly.

The ultimate responsibility of everyone and everything is on you. Make sure the people under you have everything they need to fully perform their duties, including any type of resource or training they need. When you fulfill your duties as a leader, it puts the people under you in a better position to reduce errors, and then there is no need to blame anyone for anything.

There are a lot of people in leadership positions today who have never learned how to be a leader. Some became leaders as a natural progression in their career, others forced their way into it, and some were thrown in there because they knew someone. But they don't know what it is to be a leader and yet they are pressured to perform. I liken this to an individual who has no auto mechanic experience or knowledge, but is put on the spot to fix a car that broke down while carrying a pregnant woman on her way to the hospital to deliver her baby. The individual is surrounded by a crowd of people shouting, "Fix it! Fix it!" while the pregnant woman is screaming in pain in the back seat. Most people would cave under this kind of pressure, panic, and end up making irrational decisions. This is why some leaders act the way they do. If you have ever found yourself in this situation, I want you to know that you can still learn.

An area where certain leaders struggle, especially those in the government, is in thinking that they own the position they are in. They think that they can remain there for as long as they want, regardless of the law. You must instead think of yourself as a custodian of that position. Your time there is temporary. You are to do the best that you can do while you are there; when your time is up, you must pass it on to the next person. **Even though your time on the job is temporary, if you do a good enough job, your work there will last forever.**

As a leader, the job you do will be measured by your results. The good thing about this is that you do not need to be on the job for 100 years to achieve good results; you can achieve good results in a reasonable amount of time. Choose what you focus on and making sure you excel in it. **Results outweigh any claims or promises that you could possibly make.** So no matter the promises you might have made, if you do not deliver with results, it will all count for nothing.

Sooner or later, a leader who is solely looking out for his own personal interests will be exposed. When a leader learns to combine the interests of his people with his own, everyone is better served. Everyone's interests are taken care of, making the leader's job easier.

As a leader, you are the voice of those who do not have one. You will speak up for them when they cannot be heard. You are power for the people who are powerless. When they are down and have nothing left in them to continue, you will rise up and help them through. As a leader, you give hope for those who are hopeless. When people think it is over and there is nothing else to be done, you are there to let them know it is not over yet.

If you are in a position of leadership and you are reading this, pay close attention to what I am about to tell you: Somehow, it is possible that through the actions of those who came before you, the meaning of your position has been forgotten. It's possible that the people that you lead have also forgotten what it means to have a true leader. But it's time for someone to restore the confidence of good leadership. It's time for someone to show them the true meaning of leadership. The change can start with you. Through your actions, people can believe again. Now go out and be the great leader that you were meant to be. You have it in you to be one.

CHAPTER 16: PERSONALITY AND CHARACTER

He who stands for nothing will fall for anything.
—Alexander Hamilton

What do you stand for? What are your core values? Most people live their lives without any defining principles, living a carefree life. But to be a great leader or to even become successful, you must stand for something. You must have certain principles and values that represent who you are and that you are ready to defend. If you are currently in a position where you do not have any, develop some. Commit to what you are about and what you stand for, otherwise you'll feel exposed and liable to fall for anything that comes at you.

Your values are characterized by the principles and standards by which you live that you hold dearly. All your life experiences thus far have shaped your values today, including experiences you've had with your family, education, religion, work, culture, and friends. We all react differently to experiences and situations in life, which help develop different values in each of us. You must decide which values are important to *you*. The first step is identifying what your core values are today. From the core values that you identify, determine which ones are worth holding on to and which ones don't serve you. Then identify the important values that you're missing in your life and that you need to develop.

Developing a new set of values in your life starts with self-evaluation of where you are and what areas of your life need to improve. Ask yourself the right questions: "What do I value? What is important to me? What do I want to stand for?" The answers to these questions will help you identify the right values to impart in your life. Once you identify the values you want to focus on, then learn about that value. Find out what it takes to integrate that value into your life. What do you need to give up? What changes would you need to make? Once you find out these things, come up with a plan to integrate the value into your life. Once that happens, you can begin to enjoy that value's rewards.

The list below is a guide to some values that you can integrate into your life. Although it's not comprehensive, this list serves as a good starting point to get you to think. Go through the list and see which values mean the most to you and those that represent a greater version of yourself. Make another list of the values you like and learn all you can about them. Do not rush; take your time with each value as you work, no matter how long it takes you to fully grasp that value. Once you've grasped one, start learning about another. You are not expected to perfect every single value. If you are not familiar with a certain value, look up the meaning in the dictionary and see if it is a value that you would like to have.

Humility	Hard work	Honesty
Loyalty	Patience	Peacefulness
Kindness	God-fearing	Accountability
Cleanliness	Determination	Diligence
Excellence	Honor	Obedience
Prudence	Sympathy	Truth
Generosity	Family	Innovation
Intelligence	Punctuality	Confidence

As you establish your core values and principles, you must stay away from taking any action that is not in line with those values. Instead, identify the actions that support your values. Take these actions consistently as you use them to build up your values; then the values are reinforced in your life and will ultimately make up your character. Once those values become ingrained, others around you will be able to tell what your values are by your actions and the type of person you are. This also lets them know how to approach you regarding matters that pertain to your values. If they approach you the right way, it prevents a situation where your important principles and values are violated. In the long run, this is good for you and them.

When you have the right set of values, they serve as a guide for you to make the right decisions. This is achieved when you apply your values to different situations that come up. The right set of values will prevent you from behaving badly and from making foolish choices. A highly developed values system is like a compass. It serves as a guide to point you in the right direction when you are lost.

Your character and the core values you develop greatly affect your chances of success in whatever you do. You must build up your character in the right way to improve your chances of success. All successful people and great leaders have a set of values by which they live—you can learn a lot from these leaders. By examining the character of these people, you can identify the values that they hold highly. A thorough examination allows you to see the values that have made them the successful people and the great leaders they are. Once you have identified those values, go through them and determine those you would like to apply to greatly improve the quality of your life and make you as successful or as great of a leader as they are.

When you become a great leader or as successful as you want to be, the right personality and character is needed to sustain these positions. If you don't have the right personality and character, the success you've obtained will most likely slip away from you.

Your success also depends on your ability to attract people to you. To do this, you yourself must be attractive, not physically, but through your personality and character. A lot of success in life depends on your ability to be attractive and thereby attract people to you. In the same way, your personality and your character are a big part of what people look at when deciding to do business with you. If you have a questionable character or an unpleasant personality, then people won't want to deal with you, causing you to miss out on valuable opportunities.

Since interacting with others is pertinent to your success, make sure that your personality and character are in line with someone that is worthy of establishing a relationship with. People judge your character primarily by how you act, not so much about what you say. Choose your actions carefully; make certain that what you say matches what you do. If you believe you are an honest person, then you must act honestly. Likewise, if you believe you are a truthful person, then you must be truthful. Your actions alone should communicate who you are. From your actions, people should be able to say, "This is a person of upstanding character. This is a person of high-level principles and a person whom I respect."

Generally, people with good personalities and good character are trusted through their reputations. This is a significant advantage and a position you want to be in when it comes to discovering opportunities. It increases your chances of forming quality relationships, which in turn contribute to your success. A reputation like this can completely set you apart from others around you. People will be able to tell that there is something different about you and that you are unlike the other people they do not want to deal with.

Work on developing good people skills like listening. Most people have the tendency to talk much more than they listen. Learn how to become an effective listener. If you are too busy talking and not listening, you might miss valuable information that can contribute to your success. You can also learn more by listening. You already know what you already know, so you are not necessarily learning more by talking. By listening to what others say, you are putting yourself in a position to absorb new information and possibly learn new things from that person.

Be sincere with yourself. Make sure that the person that you are portraying is in line with your real self. The people around you are not stupid; they can always detect those trying to be someone they are not. Be consistent with who you are. In your attempt to deceive others, you will only end up deceiving yourself. Be true to yourself and who you are on the inside. If you need to work on the person you are on the inside, then do so. When you do this, the person on the outside will eventually become the person you want to be.

When you do the right thing, do it because it is a part of your character and who you are, not because others are watching. If you only do good things because others are watching, you are less likely to do them when no one is watching. **You true character is tested and proven by the actions you take when there is no one watching.** This is when the true you comes out. When there is nobody present, do the right thing because it is who you are.

Life will throw different character tests at you that are designed to see how well you do. The key to passing these tests is having the right values in place that you've developed over time and that now define your character. These tests will expose the areas where you are lacking and confirm the areas in which you are already strong. If you are lacking in any way or your character is not where it needs to be, the tests and challenges you face will help shape and build up your character to what it needs to be. They are, in fact, preparing you for the next level. The challenges also build up your maturity level and prepare you should similar things happen again in the future. When you have the right character, it doesn't matter what test life throws at you; you will be ready to withstand it.

Learn to maintain a positive attitude at all times. Doing so will bring you much more happiness in life. We always have a choice in how we feel—when you make that choice, choose to be positive. Do not choose to be sad and miserable. Even in failures and disappointments, learn to find the positive side. If you look hard enough, there is a chance that some good can be found. When you find it, focus on it, and it will change how you feel inside and how you feel about the overall situation.

A positive attitude can be very infectious. People are drawn to those with positive attitudes or outlooks on life because, internally, that is how they want to feel, too. So when they see that you have something they would like to have, it brings them closer to you. Your positivity attracts them. A pleasing personality allows others to see you in a favorable way and it attracts them to you. A negative attitude, on the other hand, will repel people. Nobody wants to be around someone who is always complaining and in a bad mood. When you effuse positivity, however, you attract people to you. By attracting others to you, you can form quality relationships that can impact your chances of success. Even if you are someone known for being negative toward others, you can still change how you are perceived. As you begin to change to a more positive attitude, they too will begin to display a more positive attitude toward you and eventually your reputation will change to that of a positive person.

By maintaining a positive attitude, your chances of obtaining a better result increases because a negative attitude prevents you from seeing certain things while a positive attitude allows you to see much more. With a positive attitude, it is like you're hoping for the best in something and are therefore more likely to see more and subsequently the best in it. With a negative attitude, it is like you are hoping for the worst and are therefore more likely to see the worst in it. It is part of human nature to see more of what we focus on. Focus on the positive and you will see more of it in your life.

CHAPTER 17: DEVELOPING RELATIONSHIPS

Everything you want in life is a relationship away.

If you think about the fact that whatever you want in life, someone has access to it or knows someone else who does, then you can better understand the phrase, "Everything you want in life is a relationship away." There is someone out there that can help you get whatever you want. To get it, sometimes all you have to do is connect with the right person. The right relationships can bring you wisdom, joy, jobs, money, business contracts, happiness, influence, and anything else. This relationship could be in the form of a business relationship, family relationship, or any other form. Some of the ways to build long-lasting relationships are by being respectful, gaining mutual understanding, trust, and good communication.

Many don't take advantage of the full reach of relationships, connections, and capabilities they have because they are unaware of the people they are connected to through their network. They don't know whom their direct connections may know. When you know whom they know, though, you can tap into the entire network. If you want to find out the full reach of a relationship, simply ask the person you know directly whom they know. You can even get more specific about geography, occupation, interests, political affiliations, religion, and education. If you do not ask, you may never get to know the full extent of the possibilities available. Do not limit yourself only to the relationships that you have.

A good way to build personal relationships is through the process of self-disclosure and inquiry. Self-disclosure involves you telling someone information about yourself that can help him or her better understand who you are. If you are trying to build a deep relationship, what you tell the person must go beyond the surface level. You do not have to reveal all your secrets, but the information you share must be substantive. An example of surface-level information is your name or the type of job you do. Examples of a more substantive level of information would be information about your family or what your personal goals are. The type or amount of information you share about yourself depends on the occasion and varies from person to person.

The inquiry process, on the other hand, involves asking questions of the person with whom you are trying to build a relationship. Ask specific questions that will yield more information about that person. The answers you get from those questions will help you develop a good understanding of what that person is all about. An inquiry can also help you find out what you have in common with that person. Commonalities are great talking points that encourage communication and also build rapport. Tailor your questions around the feedback you get from that person. As you and the person exchange information about one another through the self-disclosure and the inquiry process, you will naturally develop a relationship.

There are certain people who like to lie or trick their way into relationships, but **a relationship built on lies and trickery will not last; only truthfulness can uphold a relationship.** This people will eventually be discovered and must face the consequences of their actions. This applies to any kind of relationship and the consequences they could face are up to the full extent of the law. A politician who lies his way into office will face the consequences of doing so, as will the business person who lies his way into a deal, and, similarly, a partner who lies his or her way into a marriage will also face consequences. Relationships built on truthfulness are much more secure and productive, creating an open channel for both individuals to freely communicate with each other based on trust. It also allows individuals to work better together and fully explore the possibilities of their relationship.

For a relationship to work properly, the commitment of all individuals involved is required. Everyone must put in their effort to make the relationship work. You can always tell the difference between relationships that only have one person committed and ones where everyone involved is committed. The former relationships suffer and don't operate at the best level. Oftentimes, the person putting more effort in realizes this and pulls back out of frustration. When this happens, the relationship breaks down and everyone loses. Take your relationships seriously and commit to doing what it takes to get the best out of each relationship you have.

It's important to be culturally aware and adaptable when dealing with people of other cultures and backgrounds. You must understand that the manner in which you do things and what you consider as normal might not be normal for everyone. Your way of doing things is not necessarily the right way or the only way. Africa is blessed with people of many cultures and of many different perspectives. The quicker you recognize this and acknowledge it appropriately, the easier it is for you to build relationships.

Recognizing the differences in people is very important. You can't try to fit everyone into a box or single personality type. Although we are attracted to people who talk like us, who think like us, or are like us in other ways, not everyone is like us. There are many benefits to our differences. They allow us to draw from different opinions, skill sets, ideas, and resources. To truly succeed, refrain from not liking someone or refusing to work with that person just because they are not like you.

When you compare Africans to others outside the continent, the cultural differences are staggering. In Africa, for example, much emphasis is placed on respecting individuals who are older than you. This same level of respect is expected to be given to people of high position and high authority. It also applies to social interactions between a parent and a child, teacher and student, employer and employee, and so on. While it is important to give respect where it is due, other cultures view certain aspects of the way Africans go about it all differently.

For example, while growing up in Nigeria, I was told not to look into the eyes of those older than me as a sign of respect. While conversing with a teacher or someone much older than me, I was categorically told by the individual not to look into his or her eyes. It was considered rude and disrespectful. I grew up thinking this was a normal way of life.

In my early years in America, I continued to do the same thing. But in America, and most western cultures, looking into the eyes of someone older than you or a superior at the workplace is not considered a challenge to their authority or as being disrespectful. When you meet someone, you are expected to give them a firm handshake and to make eye contact with the individual. Not making eye contact is interpreted as lacking self-confidence and a sign of weakness.

Making eye contact during a conversation is also interpreted as showing interest in what others are saying. People feel more appreciated and connected to you when you look into their eyes. Showing interest also makes them feel more valued and helps you build a deeper relationship with the individual. It was only after I understood the differences between both cultures that I was able to adapt my behavior.

In a culturally diverse continent such as Africa, cultural adaptability is an important skill to learn and practice. It's extremely difficult to be successful if you don't learn how to interact appropriately with people from different backgrounds and cultures. Cultural adaptability helps you improve your daily interactions with people and also helps you build long-lasting relationships, which are both essential to your success. Below are some of the ways to build strong relationships and to display cultural adaptability:

Be Open-Minded

Always try to have an open mind when dealing with others. Do not judge people because you've heard something about them from someone else. Do not judge people just because of their place of origin or birth. Do not assume that every person from a particular tribe acts a certain way or that they are all the same. Give everyone an opportunity to show you who they are. Engage them in conversations and ask questions so you can get a better understanding of what they stand for.

Learn Words or Phrases in Other Languages

Learning to communicate to someone in his or her language is a great way to connect. It also makes the person with whom you are communicating feel appreciated—it shows your willingness to learn about his or her culture. Even if you don't get the words or the pronunciation right, the fact that you are willing to make an effort will mean a lot to that person.

Learn About the History of Other Cultures

Educating yourself will help you make better-informed decisions and understand why people act a certain way and respond to situations differently. Before quoting or making a statement about somebody else's culture, get your facts right. Make sure you learn about his or her culture through the proper channels and not just from what somebody else said or from a source that cannot be trusted.

Be Respectful

Don't talk down to others about their ways and how they do things. Even if you have legitimate reasons to think there are better ways to do something, there are respectful ways to communicate this without offending the person to whom you are talking. Communicate with respect.

Do Not Impose Your Way on Others

It's common for most people to feel that their way of doing things is the best way. Your way of doing things might not necessarily be the best way, even if you think otherwise. If you have a better way of doing things, share your ideas with others respectfully. Avoid coming off as though you were giving an ultimatum where things either get done according to the way you do things or no way at all.

By appreciating others' cultures, you empower them, helping them feel better about who they are while boosting their confidence. When exploring other cultures, naturally you will pick certain things up consciously or unconsciously. Always exercise sound judgment and be careful about not blindly following what someone else does. The goal is not to violate your own principles or character, but rather to be culturally educated and form an educated opinion of others based on your own personal interactions. If you do this well, you will grow as a person, develop new relationships, and deepen the existing relationships that you already have.

CHAPTER 18: RESILIENCE

Sometimes it is good to be in uncomfortable situations because it is in finding our way out of such difficulties that we learn valuable lessons.

I have been fortunate in my life to meet people from all around the world. Some I have met while traveling to other countries, and others I have met while living in America. America is known as the melting pot of all nations, and it is easy to meet people from all over the world. During my university studies in America, I worked in the international admissions office, which was responsible for retaining and attracting students from all over the world to study at the university. While working there, I got a chance to interact regularly with students from different countries all over the world, some of which were places I had never imagined meeting people from. After all my interactions, I am fully convinced that Africans as a whole are some of the most resilient people in the world. I am in no way implying that all Africans are resilient, but in my experience, it is a common trait among many Africans.

Africans live and work in some of the toughest and most challenging conditions that I have ever seen or heard of. These conditions would break the average person if exposed to them. And yet, African people still wake up each day across the continent to face their struggles. Some conditions pose significant threats to their lives and basic functioning, but people continue to bounce back. This resilience is worthy of praise.

When coaching people, I try to build them up so they are more resilient. I tell them what resilience is all about and how to develop it. I also show them how it can improve their performance at work, their personal life, and all other endeavors. With most Africans, though, I do not have to do this as much because the foundation is already there.

Living in Africa teaches you how to survive, no matter where you are. There are moments in life where only the strong at heart and the well prepared will survive, and Africa definitely tests those boundaries. My focus when working with

Africans is helping them build on the resilience they already have, reinforcing the value of the trait and helping them fully understand how to apply it. If you already possess this trait, you should be encouraged for having developed it and also recognize that you have it. Your focus should now be on understanding how to use it. Focus on tapping into its power when you need it. When you know and understand what you have, you are better able to put it to use effectively. For that reason, I want to help you identify and build on what you already have and show you the role it plays in achieving success.

If you don't consider yourself to be resilient, I want you to read on as well. You will learn how you can develop resilience and to effectively apply it to your life. Most importantly, know that you do not necessarily have to live in a tough environment in order to become resilient—you can build resilience wherever you are. Being resilient is about your state of mind, not about a particular location. It is about how you react to things and how you handle yourself when faced with certain situations.

Resilience is one of the major ingredients of success, whether it is in your health, your work, at school, or at play. To be successful, you must be physically and mentally tough. If you are not, bad or hopeless circumstances will discourage you and cause you to give up on your way to success. But the wonderful thing about resilience is, no matter how badly life knocks you down, you always find the strength to get back up and keep going.

Resilience is about your ability to bounce back from adversity of any kind. It's also about your capacity to withstand or recover from any disturbance, misfortune, or interruption that threatens you. You can build resilience by understanding that your strength grows from your struggles. No matter how difficult your struggles are, you must look at them as part of a building process for you. It prepares you for the next time you have to face a similar struggle. The building process can be aided by finding out what lessons you can learn from the situations that you find yourself in. Apply these lessons to your life and position yourself to grow from the struggles you face. Note that as you go through your struggles, keep moving forward and making progress, even if only a little at a time. Every step in the right direction counts.

Resilient people know that failing at something is not necessarily the end of it. **Failure is constructive feedback that tells you to try a different approach to accomplish what you want.** A great example of this is the story of Thomas Edison. He was an avid inventor with many patents to his name. It is said that when Thomas Edison was trying to perfect the incandescent light bulb, he failed over and over until he found a way that finally worked. His attitude toward the failed attempts was not one of failure, but rather of learning. Each "failure" taught him a lesson about getting the result he wanted. This is a fantastic attitude to have. Each attempt that did not work was an invitation to try things in a different way to get the result he wanted. How many times do you try things before you quit? Are you sometimes so scared of failure that you cannot summon the courage to make an attempt at something? Thomas Edison never quit. He was not scared of failing, either. He kept trying over and over again until he achieved success.

When people fail at something sometimes, they take it personally and call themselves a failure. But they didn't fail—the approach they took failed. Instead of calling yourself a failure, try things in a different way. If that way does not work, try another one. Each approach that does not work can teach you a valuable lesson. Learn and grow from them—you will get better with each try, just as you learn from your mistakes. One thing that is certain is that it is difficult for failure to remain in the way of a determined mind that keeps on trying. Sometimes you just have to keep going until you "fail your way to success," just as Thomas Edison did.

Below are some quotes from Thomas Edison to give you an insight into his mindset and the type of person he was:
- "Our greatest weakness lies in giving up. The most certain way to succeed is to try just one more time."
- "Negative results are just what I want. They're just as valuable to me as positive results. I can never find the thing that does the job best until I find the ones that don't."

People without resilience fall apart when bad things happen to them. They are easily broken and often feel like victims when things go the wrong way. They feel powerless, but when you are resilient, you can tap into your inner strength. By applying that inner strength, you can stay resilient through rough times. Resilience helps you overcome adversity and bounce back from a setback. It also helps you to stay persistent through your struggles.

Resilience also helps you become more aware of the different support structures available to you. Most people avoid getting into a struggle or hanging in there long enough to find out what support structures are available to them. Often, it is only when you are in such struggles that you can find these structures, which could include resources from your community, family members, and friends. They are resources that you did not know existed or were not available to you previously. Your demonstration of resilience allows you to discover these resources and to take advantage of them so they can help you overcome your struggles.

Developing and maintaining a positive attitude is a great way to build your resilience. A positive attitude gives you willpower to keep going, irrespective of what you have been through. A positive attitude makes you stronger and more resilient toward the things that you face. When you have a positive attitude, you see the good, and not the bad. When you have a positive attitude, you also act differently from others because you are motivated to take action from a positive place.

One of the most remarkable demonstrations of the power of a positive attitude and resilience is the famous story of Nelson Mandela. He spent a huge portion of his life in prison. While in prison, he continued to maintain a positive attitude and belief that he would be free one day. By exercising resilience, he was able to overcome all the adversity he faced. After twenty-seven years, he was finally freed—and he eventually rose to become the president of South Africa. When he became president, he could have easily used his power to retaliate against those who jailed him, but he instead decided to maintain a positive attitude. Few people would act in the same way. Most people, after spending just a month in prison, would eagerly retaliate, but Nelson Mandela maintained a positive attitude and exemplified some of the highest human standards. For those reasons, he will forever remain an icon for all.

Another way to develop resilience is through parenting. Parents can teach their children how to be resilient by showing them good examples. Parents should also emphasize the importance of being resilient, the role that it plays in their children's everyday lives, and how it contributes to their success. Teachers can also inform children about resilience in the classroom and in all the other activities they participate in outside the classroom. The goal for both parents and teachers is to teach the children resilience while they are young so they can develop it at a young age and benefit from it for the rest of their lives.

The strong desire to succeed can build resilience as well. This desire will keep you feeling empowered to proceed, regardless of what you come up against. It keeps you going and fighting for what you want, even when you feel like quitting. The desire for success can also be driven by your belief in the meaning behind your actions. When you believe in what you do, it empowers you to commit yourself and ensure success. If you ever find that you're unable to commit yourself to something or do not feel motivated by it, try finding the meaning behind what you are doing. Find something in it you can believe in and your attitude will change. Your belief in its meaning will make the effort and commitment worthwhile.

People always talk about being comfortable in life. **But a good portion of the things you want in life is outside your comfort zone. You must stretch and push yourself beyond this zone to obtain those things.** No matter how out of reach they seem, as long as you are determined, you will find a way to achieve what you want. Maybe you are used to sleeping ten hours a day to maintain your level of comfort, but you might now have to start sleeping six hours or less a day to achieve your goals. Maybe you are only comfortable working ten hours a week on your dream, but you might now have to start working twenty hours a week to make it come true. Sometimes you are required to step outside your comfort zone and daily routine to get the life that you really want. From this day forth, challenge yourself by pushing your limits and operating on the edge of your abilities. **Stretch yourself beyond your comfort zone so that you can be all that you are capable of being.**

Always try to be resilient whenever the situation calls for it. You'll find that whenever you choose to be resilient, you'll discover new talents and abilities within you that you never knew existed. It might be tough to do this at times, but find a way to stay resilient and it will bring out the best in you. Be courageous and hopeful in your dealings; adapt to the situations that you come across. These things will help you stay resilient through the circumstances you face so that you can eventually overcome them. After all, whether you know it or not, you were built to triumph over these things. You are an overcomer. Think of yourself as such, and you will be so. It will summon the power within you to be resilient.

CHAPTER 19: TIME MANAGEMENT

There are only twenty-four hours in a day. This is the same for everyone, regardless of who you are or what your status is. It doesn't matter if you are the president of a nation, the richest man in the world, an Olympic gold medal-winning athlete, or a university professor; we all have twenty-four hours in a day. Your respect for time and how you chose to spend it is what makes the difference with each individual. Some choose to spend their time wisely and gain results while others waste their time and have nothing to show for it. In either case, the clock keeps on ticking. It never stops and every second that goes by is gone forever. For this reason, time is one of the most precious commodities there is.

Time is so important that many cultures around the world value time much more importantly than they value money. But both are related. I'm sure you have heard the expression "Time is money" before. This is so because you need time to make money. If time is money, then you have to take time as seriously as you take money. You have to manage your time wisely. The returns for time and money are also similar. Just like managing your money wisely can yield more money, managing your time wisely can also yield more time. If you don't manage your time wisely, that time would be lost and you will have nothing to show for it. The same thing goes with your money.

To be successful in life, you must take time seriously. If you don't, you might miss the opportunity of a lifetime. The problem with this is that you might never get a second chance to regain the lost opportunity. As the saying goes, time waits for no man, so you shouldn't expect an opportunity to wait for you. You have to show up on time every time so that good opportunities don't pass you by. Now, if you happen to show up on time but the opportunity does not come, then that is fine; you were prepared and on time. I personally like to make it a point to show up even before the opportunity does so that when it eventually comes, I am ready to pounce on it. When the opportunity comes up, I don't want to be rambling around, trying to figure out what to do with it. My actions are also based on my understanding that **opportunity does not waste**

time with those who are unprepared. Apart from the unprepared, opportunity does not waste time with those who are too slow to recognize it or to take advantage of the opportunity. If you're not ready when it shows up, eventually it will move on. When opportunity comes, you have to act on it.

Many things fight for our attention in this world today, everything from the television, radio, Internet, cellphones, and the people around you. So it's important that you learn how to control what you pay attention to. **Where your attention goes, your time goes.** Be mindful of this if you're going to be efficient with your time. Every second counts. There is an opportunity cost for every piece of time that you spent unproductively. Every second that you spend on something unimportant amounts to valuable time being wasted. Identifying the time-wasters in your life and choose to ignore them. They come in the form of both people and activities and they don't help you get anything accomplished. They are people who talk to you all day about unimportant things and don't allow you the time to work on the things you need to get done. Time-wasting activities also take your time away from important things that need to get done. By identifying who and what they are and getting rid of these distractions, you can take control of your time.

Most people think that if they could only have more time, they would get all their pressing things done. But instead of asking for more time, what they should do is learn to make better use of the time they already have. If they manage their time better, their lives will improve. Some of the ways in which you can better manage your time is by getting organized and learning to do things more efficiently. Simplify things for yourself by removing any clutter that exists in your life and you will notice a difference in your efficiency.

Two particular strategies in managing time more efficiently include the "80/20 rule," also known as the Pareto Principle, and the other is Parkinson's Law. Both of these, when applied to your life in the right way, can greatly improve your ability to manage your time effectively.

In the 1900s, the economist Vilfredo Pareto made an amazing discovery in his native Italy: 20 percent of the population owned 80 percent of the land. This left the remaining 20 percent of the land to be distributed among the remaining 80 percent of the population. He later noticed that the distribution was the same in every country he surveyed. Since his discovery, others have observed similar things and the 80/20 rule has been applied to different areas such as sales, business management, and so on. When applying the 80/20 rule to time management, it is believed that 80 percent of your results come from 20 percent of your activities. That means that only a few things you do give you the biggest results. For example, if you have ten things to do on your schedule on any given day, two of those things will give you a higher degree of results than the other eight things would. If you really want to be efficient with your time, you have to put your best efforts into the two things that give you the biggest results.

The 80/20 rule also applies to things that fight for your attention and your time. To repel time-wasters, remind yourself of the 20 percent of activities on which you must focus. That 20 percent becomes your highest priority because it has highest impact on your results. If you ever run into a situation where you won't finish everything you need to get done, make sure that the things that you do finish are part of the 20 percent, as they will make the biggest difference.

The idea behind working on the 20 percent is to help you save time. This doesn't mean that you should always ignore the other 80 percent of your work. You are responsible for all 100 percent of your work; it's not complete till it's all done. This rule is purely a time-saving technique.

You have already been introduced to Parkinson's Second Law, which we applied earlier to the wisdom of money. This law will be discussed here as it applies to time management. Introduced by a man named Cyril Northcote Parkinson, the law states that work expands so as to fill the time available for its completion, which means that if you set a goal to complete a task in a month, you will complete it in a month. If you set the same goal to complete the task in three months, you will complete it in three months. The amount of time that it takes you to finish a task expands in direct proportion to the amount of time you give yourself to finish that task. This is so even if the same task could have been completed in five days. When you know you have extra time, you adjust the pace of your work to match up with that time. You start to take on additional research, slow your work rate, or add on extra steps to prolong the process of completing the task. You essentially look for things to do to fill in the extra time that you have. This can be a very tricky trap, though, as you could end up spending more time working on a task than you needed. You can, however, effectively manage your time and avoid this trap.

The trick to time-efficiency is to approach a task as though you have very little time to complete it. Instead of giving yourself a month to work on the task, give yourself two weeks instead. Proceed with the task, making sure to act and think like the shortened amount of time is all that you have. This will help you focus on completing the task and it will also cut down on any unnecessary time wastage. By setting time limits, your mind will work for you and find a way to finish the task within the shortened amount of time.

There is a common practice among many Africans known as the "African time." It is characterized by a disregard for time, often marked by showing up late to an event or appointment several hours after the event started. It has gotten so bad that certain event planners and organizers actually factor it in when planning for an event. So if they start an event at 5 p.m., for example, they tell people the event starts at 3 p.m. Even the organizers arrive late.

The saddest part of the "African Time" practice is that it is all based on what people believe others will do. The majority of those who show up late only do so because they believe others will show up late, too. Hence, they don't want to be the first to get there or one of the few people at the event who waits for everyone else to show up. This tells me it is actually possible for everyone to get to the event on time. If everyone just stopped thinking about what others will do, then this problem can be solved. If each person does the right thing and shows up on time, then everyone will be there on time.

The notion that it is acceptable to be intentionally late to an event is completely unacceptable. **You should not be intentionally late to an event just so you can match up with others' displays of poor judgment.** It is equally worse to do it just because "everyone else is doing it." Set high standards for yourself. Remember: You are a leader in your own right. Make your own decisions based on what you know is right. Let others make their own bad decisions if they choose to. As a leader, you must set the right examples and not follow others' bad examples. If you are scheduled to be somewhere at a particular time, be there on time. I once heard someone say that if you arrive at an event five minutes before it is supposed to start, you are already late. That is the mentality you need to have. Give yourself enough time to make up for any unplanned events that might delay you from arriving on time.

The power to curb the problem of "African time" lies with the people. When you arrive late somewhere, you are actually disrespecting others' time. You are actually saying, "My time is more important than yours and so I will show up whenever I feel like it; I don't care if you have to wait for me." It still goes on because people tolerate and celebrate it. When people start condemning it for what it is, then it will stop. When people accept that it has a negative effect on everyone's productivity and drags down the growth of Africa, then it will stop. The solution lies within everyone collectively. The people have to come together to say no to it. Everyone has to agree to live by a higher standard and to hold each other accountable.

Learning to respect time and manage it wisely will do you an enormous amount of good. It will contribute to your success in more ways than you know. Time management is not just about finding things to keep you busy, but also to learn how to be productive with your time. To this, continuously ask yourself: "Am I making the best use of my time right now? Am I spending my time where I am supposed to be spending it?" The answers to those questions will help keep you on track.

Develop a sense of urgency in your work. Do it in a way that maximizes your time, leaving no room for unnecessary time wastage. Regardless of what you are doing, always make sure you get the important things done. **When it comes to the important things, it's not about finding time to get them done—it's about making time to get them done.** There is a big difference between finding time and making time. When you make time, you give it priority so that something gets done. Above all, remember that **time**

management is about life management. When you manage your time well, you will manage your life well.

CHAPTER 20: WHAT WOULD "THEY" THINK? WHAT WOULD "THEY" SAY?

Due to the close-knit nature of African society, it is easy to feel deeply connected to the people around you. By nature, you feel accountable to those you are connected to and it manifests itself in your thoughts and actions. This feeling also causes you to worry about what others think about you and what you are doing at any given point in time. "They" refers to a list of people whose opinions matter to you. For most people, there is no physical list of names written down anywhere; it is a mental list that exists only in their heads. "They" are all kinds of people, including friends, teachers, uncles, aunts, neighbors, co-workers, parents, and others. For some people, the list could have 20 names on it, and for others it could have as many as 100 names. There is no minimum or maximum amount of people that could be on the list. It varies from person to person depending on their interactions with others and the quality of the relationship they have with these individuals.

Whenever we think about doing something, we immediately refer to this list. We ask ourselves, "What would they think?" or "What would they say?" As we ask ourselves these questions, we can picture these people in our heads looking at us. As we think of each person, we unconsciously start to shape our behavior to what we think that person would expect from us. If it is something that we are thinking of doing, we veer away from doing it when we realize that one person we are thinking of may not approve of it. If it is something that we have already done and we know the people on our list would not approve of it, we feel guilt and disgust for doing what we did. When we feel this way, we immediately try to find a way to reverse what we did.

The feeling of guilt and disgust gets stronger and stronger depending on how highly we value the opinion of the person we picture in our head. If it is someone we value a lot, we feel really bad about ourselves. If it is someone we don't value as much, we feel a bit less bad about ourselves. Our subsequent thoughts and actions are also affected based on how strong our feelings are and how much we value that person. If he or she is someone we value a lot, the thought of that person might cause us to immediately stop what we're doing. If he or she is someone we don't value as much, it might take us a bit longer to decide on what action to take.

The person or people we think of on the list depend on the specific situation we are evaluating. As a result, different people come to mind for different situations. As an example, you may think of your parents if you are thinking of skipping a class at school or of your dad if you did not do well on a test. Your parents have always told you to go to class and never skip it; for that reason, you think of them when you are thinking of skipping class. The person you think of depends on the corresponding associations you have formed in your head about that person and what you are doing.

Evaluate how the people on your list make you feel. If some people make you feel and react positively, then by all means keep them on your list. If some make you work hard toward your goals, keep them on your list. If some on your list make you more respectful toward others, keep them on your list. If some make you do better at school than you usually would, keep them on your list. As long as those people influence you positively, they should remain on your list. Their positive influence leads to your positive actions, which give you positive results.

A big problem, though, is that sometimes we put certain people on the list that shouldn't be there because they negatively affect our behavior and encourage us to do the wrong things. When we think of them as we ask ourselves, "What would they think?" or "What would they say?" we justify doing those wrong things in our head. Since we don't want to feel less than adequate in their eyes, we do the wrong thing, even though we know, deep down in our hearts, that it's wrong. These people on our list encourage us to be lazy, tell lies, get into fights, steal, commit fraud, and do other negative things. These are people we can certainly do without in our lives, since they only affect us in negative ways.

These people can hold you back in life; they will do this if you let them. By having them on your list, you will begin to do things according to what you think will please them. You might spend money on things that you would normally not spend money on just because of that person. People even go so far as to set life goals based on what other people want or others' goals. They may say something to the effect of, "I will choose this profession because this person will admire me for it." When they do this, they run the risk of doing something they really don't want to do and not being able to get any personal satisfaction out of it. You need to watch what you do for the sake of gaining others' acceptance. Watch also for people who make you do negative things by taking certain actions so you don't disappoint them.

Don't hold yourself back from success to please other people or to not disappoint them. And certainly don't hold yourself back from success because you think people won't like you anymore. It is impossible to please everybody. If you spend your whole life trying to please everyone you come into contact with, you will end up draining your energy for the wrong reasons. Conserve your energy; don't burn it up unnecessarily on such negativity.

If you have people such as these on your mental list that pressure you negatively, then you must remove them. Since you put them on your mental list in the first place, you also have the power to remove them from the list. To do this, don't think about them when you are evaluating something you are about to do. Don't think about them when you are reviewing your past actions. They don't even have to know that you removed them from your list because the list exists only in your head. You are the only one who knows who is on the list and when someone comes off the list or gets added to it. Remove them now and you can go on enjoying your life without the negative influence they have on you.

Having core principles that you stand by will help protect you from others' negativity. Every great leader has a set of core principles that he or she believes in and wouldn't change for anyone, principles developed over time that have now become a part of who he or she is. These principles should be so strong that you'll never abandon them. People and situations will constantly test your core principles to see how firm they are. You must remain unshakeable, irrespective of what people say or do. If your core principles, along with your character are built up, they will help you withstand the negative influence of other people.

As a leader, remember that you cannot make all your decisions based on what people think or say about you. Instead, make decisions based on what is right and what needs to be done. If you know something is not right, do not do it. If you know it is right thing to do, then go ahead and do it. You do not need anyone's permission or approval to do what is right for you. You can make your own decisions.

To overcome any problems that you might have around this, work on your ability to make firm decisions. This is a good skill to have because when you have problems with making decisions, your inability to do so could cause you a lot of confusion and stress that may negatively impact your body and mind. Have confidence in yourself—confidence comes from knowledge. If you are knowledgeable about what you are doing, you'll have the confidence you need to make decisions and take appropriate action. With that in mind, try to learn as much as you can about what you are doing. This will help you make confident decisions.

You cannot live your entire life solely based on what you think other people would think or say about you. If you do, you will wake up one day only to find out that you have been living someone else's life, not yours. Get busy living your own life. Develop an identity of your own. **Do not minimize the person you are by burying your personality just because of what people will think or say about you.** You cannot afford to lose your personal identity in trying to satisfy others. If I had lived my life completely based on what everyone else thought or said about me, I would have failed a long time ago. I would not have made some of the decisions I made, which turned out to be the right decisions for my life.

No one can control your thoughts or make you feel a certain way unless you allow them to. You hold the key and only you can give access to anyone to make you feel a certain way. No matter what they think or what they say, it does not affect you unless you allow it to. You are in total control. Make wise choices and think thoroughly about your decisions before you make them, irrespective of what anyone says or thinks. Pay attention to the people that surround you and those you think about when making decisions. Make sure that they are people of high character and values. As you spend time with them and spend time thinking about them, their character and values become your character and values.

LESSON V: TRUST

Trust is at play every day in our lives. We trust that when we walk, the ground will not move away from our feet. We trust that when we breathe in, there will be oxygen in the air. We trust that when we move our hands, they will go in the direction we want them to go. We do these things without thinking or expecting otherwise.

Trust also plays a part in our relationships. For a marriage to succeed, both spouses must trust each other. For a friendship to succeed, both friends must trust each other. Trust plays a role in our daily interactions with people and in forming strong relationships. The degree of trust needed for each individual relationship to succeed may vary from relationship to relationship, but there has to be some form of trust present.

Building trust should be something that you do intentionally. Since you know that trust is a necessary ingredient for a relationship to succeed, make it a priority to develop it. Doing this allows you to fully enjoy the benefits that come with that relationship. Trustworthy people are usually considered more reliable. People count on them more and feel more confident about the promises they make. Since they are considered more reliable, it is only natural that they develop stronger and more lasting connections. Those connections in turn lead to more opportunities.

Each of us has something I like to call the trust scale. It's a way to measure the level of trust that you have for someone at any given time. The level at which you put someone on the trust scale determines how much you trust them. When you first meet someone, you unconsciously assign that person a starting point on your trust scale, which varies from person to person. Each individual has his or her own unique set of factors to use in deciding the starting level on the trust scale. These factors are all in your head, including such things as your prior experience with people in general, the nature of the environment in which you reside, your perception of the person to whom you are assigning a level on your trust scale, the circumstances in which you met that person, and several other factors.

Positions on your trust scale are not fixed. If someone betrays your trust in any way, they drop down on the scale, depending on what they did. For example, if someone betrays your trust in a very small way, the drop in the trust scale might be minimal, perhaps small enough that it doesn't affect your interactions with that person. But if a person significantly betrays you, he or she could drop all the way down your trust scale to zero. At this level, you have absolutely no trust in this person. You become skeptical about everything the person does.

The level a person is on the scale also determines how much attention you pay to their actions. Your primary reason for doing this is to protect yourself from that person. For someone high up on your trust scale, you might start off not watching them at all. If that person drops down a little, you may, figuratively speaking, start to watch him or her with "one eye open." If that person drops even farther down your trust scale, you begin to pay more attention with "both eyes wide open." If that person drops even farther down your trust scale, then your next step is to get other people to join you in watching the individual to ensure that you don't miss anything that this person does. At this point, everything that person does is under your scrutiny.

The level a person is on your trust scale also determines what you trust that individual with and what you allow that individual to do for you. If someone is really high on your trust scale, you may trust the individual with everything. If the individual falls down, you may no longer trust the person with everything, but you could still trust the person enough to let the individual borrow money from you. If the person falls farther down the trust scale, you may no longer let the individual borrow money from you, but you may still let them borrow books from you. The bottom of your trust scale is the point where you do not trust the person with anything at all.

When someone drops all the way to the bottom, the individual is usually not condemned to that position; he or she could move up the scale again by earning back your trust. If there is someone you had a really bad experience with, the process to earn back your trust may take a bit more time and effort. In some cases, the person does not manage to get back to the level at which they once were on your trust scale. This is something that also varies from person to person. It depends on the individual's ability to forgive and to let go of the things that happened.

If you have betrayed someone else's trust, it is important for you to come to terms with what you have done. Once you have done this, the next step is to apologize to that person and let them know that you are sorry. This apology has to be sincere.

For people who have trouble trusting someone either because of a prior experience with that person or some other reason, it is possible to determine if the person is worthy of your trust again. By putting the person who betrayed your trust through a test, you can find out if that person can be trusted again. For example, if you have suspicions about someone telling your secrets, you could exclusively tell them something and then see if you hear it from others. If you do hear it elsewhere, then there is a good possibility it came from that individual, since he or she was the only person you told. Based on what you find out, you can then determine how you want to handle your relationship with this person going forward. Trust is very important; you must pay attention to how you assign your trust to people and how trustworthy you are to others. It is the basis for true, lasting relationships.

CHAPTER 21: BRANDING

What do people think of when they hear your name? What is the first thing that comes to their mind when they think of you? Are you someone people want to do business with? Do people trust you? Does your name invoke confidence? Whether you believe it or not, you already have a brand. The answers to these questions give you an idea of how you are viewed by the outside world and what your brand is. It is a common problem for people not to know what their brand is. If you fall into this category, there is good news: Not only can you find out what your brand is, but also you can most importantly shape what you want your brand to be and how you want to be viewed by others.

Knowing what your brand is allows you to know where you stand. When you know where you stand, you are better able to position yourself correctly to take advantage of opportunities as they arise. Knowing what your brand is also helps you enhance the relationships you already have and to develop new relationships. When you know exactly where you stand, you are better able to plug any gaps that you might have.

When a company is sold, a portion of the total value of the company includes something called goodwill. A company's goodwill is not a physical asset that you can touch, like an office building, automobile, or equipment. Goodwill is a value above and beyond all those assets. It refers to such things as a strong brand name, effective customer service, and a good reputation in the market. It's also about how receptive people are to a company's products and services. Most successful companies have a very high value for their goodwill. This high value is a major part of their continued success. It is also why customers continue to be attracted to the company.

Just as companies need a positive goodwill to deal with customers and expand their business, we as individuals also need a positive brand to deal with other people. If you have a reputation as being untrustworthy, then people won't want to do business with you. Trust is a key personal trait that must be a part of your brand. Like with most companies, this is one of the most valuable assets there is. Having a brand as someone that can be trusted is an important part of being successful. It greatly affects whether or not people are drawn to you.

Many years ago, I started a financial company in America that specialized in the area of wealth management that catered to the financial needs of wealthy individuals, families, and businesses. This is a highly competitive field in finance; a lot of the biggest financial companies in the world are aggressively involved in this field. A big reason for the competitiveness of this field is the large amounts of money these individuals control. A few of these individuals could make your company very successful, leaving your company with millions and millions of dollars to manage.

I have learned a lot from working with these individuals, just as they have gained from my expertise. They are people who have done really well for themselves in various disciplines such as healthcare, finance, management, technology, oil and gas, manufacturing, and so on. They are rich, well connected, and informed. Some of the biggest banks and financial services companies target them as potential customers.

I was able to compete with these gigantic companies because I understood one fundamental fact, which is that **when people TRUST you, they will deal with you, irrespective of how big or small your company is, provided you are able to meet their needs**. By earning the trust of my clients, I was able to earn their business as well. I earned their trust by showing that I was good at what I did and that I had their best interests in mind. Gaining the trust of my clients was the first thing I had to do to grow my business. If I did not have their trust, they would not deal with me and my business would not grow.

Great companies understand that they need trust from their customers to succeed, which is why they invest heavily into building trust. They put out advertisements to communicate to customers that their product or services can be trusted. The also invest heavily in maintaining customer loyalty to their brand.

When a company has a strong brand, it's easy to attract new customers and increase sales. When people see their products, they are attracted to it because they trust it and know that it will fulfill their needs. Part of the work I enjoy is helping companies understand what their brand is and helping them effectively communicate it to their clients. I also enjoy working with employees so they are on board with the plan and know how they can help fulfill the goals of the company. Companies that invest in their brand through consulting, marketing, or other means often see the rewards of doing so.

You, too, must invest in your personal brand. If there is one trait that your brand must speak of, it is trust. People have to know that you are morally sound. Having the trust of the people you deal with is crucial to your success. People should know that when they do business with you, you won't try to cheat or deceive them. People should know, for example, that if they leave you alone around their property when no one is looking, you will not steal from them. The people that cheat and steal are really short-sighted because, in the long run, they are the ones that end up losing. **The person that cannot be trusted with small things cannot be trusted with big things.** If you cheat or steal from someone today and think you have gotten away with it, the very thing you did could come back to haunt you down the road. You have to be trustworthy across the board in all things at all times. I know too many people that have missed out on the big opportunities. When they were trusted with something small, they disappointed the person that trusted them and so they were not even given a chance with something big.

Your brand should convey a clear promise with a positive message that says: "If you deal with me, this is what you will get." By maintaining a brand with a consistent promise, people should know what they will get when they deal with you. Think of designer shoes, designer clothes, or luxury car brands, for instance. These things might be expensive, but when you buy them, you have high expectations of the brands. You know they are manufactured to a higher degree of quality. You know they will perform well and that they will last longer than inferior brands. That is the kind of promise your brand should convey.

Keep a record of what you have done in the past to support this promise. It should state: "Based on my history, this is who I am, this is what I have done, and this is what you will get from me." Your actions going forward should continue to maintain that record and support your promise. Your actions should show that you are committed to maintaining your brand and intend to keep your promise.

Your brand must communicate the value that you bring to a working relationship. Your employer or manager should know what they can expect from you as an employee. He or she should know what they can trust you with. Your co-workers should also know what to expect from you as a fellow employee. They should know that they can count on you for support as needed and to do your work well. The people you do business with should know what to expect in your business relationship; let them know that they can always rely on you to keep your word and do exactly what you said you would do when you said you would do it. People that keep on promising things but never actually deliver on their word are not to be trusted. **Trust is not so much about what you say, but about what you do.** Prove that you are someone to be trusted by your actions.

When you do not make good on your promise time and time again, people will write you off and won't expect anything more from you. They no longer want to associate with you and are very careful with what they involve you in. They also may doubt everything you say. When this happens, you miss out on opportunities you might otherwise have had.

Sometimes, people know your brand before ever meeting you. Through word of mouth, people outside your circle of friends can hear about you, your brand, and what you stand for. When you are known to be trustworthy, it attracts others to you and makes you difficult to ignore. By attracting the right people to you, you can make new connections with people that will contribute to your success. If word gets around that you are not trustworthy, people will avoid you before they even meet you, and you'll miss out on the contributions they could have made toward your success.

Knowing that word gets around about your brand is good because you can use it to your advantage. When building your brand, start first with your family, friends, and those around you. Make sure they know who you are and what your values are. As you do this, they consciously or unconsciously will spread the word to others about you. As they do this, you will reap the rewards of those positive messages.

Building your brand by starting this way is a form of personal marketing, and you can influence how people see you. Personal marketing allows you to play a direct role as people form an opinion of you instead of leaving it solely to them. Sending the right messages allows you to create an image for yourself that can positively affect your future.

When marketing yourself this way, it is important to be humble. Be careful not to come off as prideful or boastful; it's a huge turnoff for a lot of people. The goal is to get others to talk about you in a positive way. Coming across as prideful or boastful won't encourage that. Most people will instead speak negatively about you, which is the opposite of the result you want.

Make sure to assess yourself. A self-assessment will help you determine what your brand is about. A thorough self-assessment will also help you examine your strengths and weaknesses as well as determine the areas of your life you need to maintain or improve upon. Go through the series of questions below and come up with quality answers that will guide you toward developing the brand you want.

Self-Assessment
1. How do people perceive me? (If you are not sure about this, ask a few people for their honest opinion.)

2. What are the strengths of my brand?

3. What can I do to maintain or improve upon my strengths?

4. What are the weaknesses in my brand?

5. What can I do to turn those weaknesses into strengths?

6. Does my brand portray trust?

7. If it does, what are some things I could do to build on that trust?

8. If it doesn't, what are some of the things I could do today to develop trust?

9. Overall, what do I want my brand to be?

10. What do I need to do to develop the brand I want for myself?

The sum total of all the values you have and display to others is what defines your brand. It's what people see; it's how they form an opinion of you. Outside of trust, there are other very important values you should have in your life. Based on your answers to the questions above, I want you to commit to doing three things every day to develop and build the brand you want. These three things should consist of actions of your own choosing that you take to display and reinforce the brand you want to build. If you do this exercise correctly, you should be on your way toward developing the brand that you want. Remember to continue to take consistent action toward building and maintaining your brand. I am fully confident that you have what it takes and you will be successful in building the brand you want.

CHAPTER 22: IT TAKES A VILLAGE

There is no power for change greater than a community discovering what it cares about.
—Margaret J. Wheatley

A popular saying goes: "It takes a village to raise a child." There is a lot of truth in this and it is a time-tested practice in Africa. The saying is about the power of a group of people working together as one. When people cooperate with each other, there is no limit to what can be achieved. Growing up in Nigeria, I had several uncles, aunts, family friends, and schoolteachers who were all collectively responsible for raising me. Every time I was in their presence, I felt like I had my parents' eyes on me. I had to act responsibly at all times, regardless of where I was, because I never knew who was around, watching me.

One time, I had gone fishing at a particularly dangerous location while my parents were away at work. When my dad got home, he asked me, "What were you doing fishing at the canal today?" With a surprised look on my face, I wondered how he knew. He was at work the whole time; there was no way he could have seen me. Unbeknownst to me, one of my neighbors had seen my friend and me earlier that morning heading to the canal with our fishing gear. I had been careful to make sure no one saw me, but apparently I did not do a good enough job. That incident told me there was always someone, somewhere, watching me wherever I was.

Such was the close-knit community I came from in Lagos. As big as it was, everyone seemed to know each other, and word got around about everything you did. My community was made up of people with very strong connections to each other. All over Africa, there are close communities of people similar to this. You or somebody you know has probably experienced something like this, too. You can find such strong connections in cities as big as Lagos and in tiny little villages you have never heard of. It is especially more common in smaller communities. A lot of these communities are made up of people with similar values, traditions, and beliefs that have been passed down from generation to generation. These people know each other really well and they are very much involved in each other's lives.

I believe this sense of community is ingrained in Africans. We have a big desire to belong to a group, a tribe, or a community. It is important to be accepted by the group; we do whatever we can to earn its acceptance and when we do, we feel loved and enjoy our interactions with other members. Being in such a group becomes part of our identity and we take immense pride in our association with it. When people ask us who we are, we say that we belong to so-and-so tribe or group. We identify ourselves by the group to which we belong.

We feel at ease around other members of our group. It's almost as if all of our problems go away when we are in their presence. We also feel safe in the numbers that the group or community has to offer us. We feel that when there are more people involved in the group, there is a greater amount of people to support us when we need it. We also feel protected and at rest with the knowledge that there is someone else out there who cares about us and is willing to look after our interests.

There is also a sense of unity built within the group when everyone works together. When everyone works toward the same cause, they all come together as one, strengthening the ability to combine all their resources and use them to their greatest effect. This further builds loyalty within the group. Everyone realizes that they are in it together and feel obligated to help each other to make things work for everyone's good.

A tight community of people is one of the few things that can provide the feelings that we seek internally. That is why people long so much to be a part of a group that may offer what they feel is missing in their lives. The internal need that people have to experience the things that a group offers, such as safety, has driven them to join all kinds of groups. Some groups they join have positive effects on them, and some do not. Groups such as certain cults and terrorist organizations do a lot of harm, not only to those who join them, but also to the people affected by their activities. Once people join these groups, they begin to think and act like the other members, supporting the cause of the group, even when in something destructive.

Beneficial to your success is a network of supporters, friends, fans, and well-wishers. They can cheer you on when you are down or feel like quitting. As they know your story and your ambitions, there is a deep connection between you and them. These individuals know where you are coming from and they know where you are going. They also help you connect the dots and assist you when you need help. It is human nature to want to repay whatever good is being done for you, and you can accomplish this by supporting others when they need help.

The community system is something that has been practiced in Africa for a long time and is still very much alive around the continent. This sense of community does not come naturally to a lot of cultures around the world, which is why Africans need to be proud of what they have. Most other cultures tend to keep to themselves and do not care as much about maintaining strong relationships with individuals in their community outside of their close circle of friends and some family members. They place their privacy and their individualism above relationships. While there might be some legitimate reasons for this in unique situations, I believe it is far more beneficial to be connected to a group of people than not. You simply cannot deny the positive effects of having a support structure and a core group of people who mean well for you.

You will be involved in many things in life that require the cooperation of other people to be successful. It is easier for you to get the cooperation you need when you already have an established group of people that you can go to when that time comes. Don't wait till you need help from people before you start to make friends with them. The last thing you want is to come off as someone who only reaches out to people when you need help. Start working on building those relationships today so you will not be found wanting in the time of need. If you wait till that time to build relationships, it may already be too late.

The sense of community that involves working together is frequently encouraged in the western world, especially in business organizations and various social groups. I like this interpretation of the acronym T.E.A.M.: "Together Everyone Achieves More." The thought of everyone working together toward the same goal makes a lot of sense and hence the reason it is so widely encouraged. There are many positives to draw from it.

Teamwork is important in the business world. It is strongly believed that a company can be more successful if all the employees work together as opposed to each person working alone. Major corporations practice this and have systems and procedures in place to guide employees toward working in a collective team effort. It is really helpful when team members possess different skill sets and are all working toward a collective goal. When it is met, everyone wins, including the company. If one team member is weak in a certain area, another team member who is strong in that area is there to make up the difference. This is a good lesson for any community to learn. **Individually, we may have weaknesses, but as a group, those weaknesses are diminished.** We become stronger when we act as one unit.

For Africa to achieve its potential for greatness, everyone must join together and work for the good of the continent. The different communities, villages, tribes, and every other type of group that exists must work together as one. Africans can no longer give their allegiance only to their tribe, but to the larger group that includes everyone. Just like the whole village joins in to raise the child, it will take a collective effort to improve the continent. **You can no longer see or identify yourself solely as a member of a tribe, but as a citizen of a nation of one people working together toward a common purpose.** When we do this, everyone achieves more.

Even though the community system has been practiced in Africa for years, people don't fully understand the power of a community acting together. They only use the power of their community in certain areas of their lives, never fully exploring the full potential that it has. I want you to know that it has the ability to do more and to influence many different areas of our lives much more than you think. **There is immense power when a group of people with similar interests gets together to work toward the same goals.** There is power to create things, power to change lives, and the power to do a lot more. I encourage you to explore the different ways that you can apply this power.

The power of the community lies in the ability to tap into the collective effort and abilities of everyone that is a part of it. A community that is engaged and working together can be a force to be reckoned with. So much can be achieved when you put everyone's individual talents together. Together, Africans can make a bigger impact wherever they choose when they work together. When everyone as a whole uses the power that exists in a community, people will no longer feel that they have to wait on the government to solve all their problems. They will instead become aware of the power that lies within them, the power to make a difference, and the power to change things for good.

To build an effective community, everyone must realize that their community is bigger than them. Each person counts and no one's voice goes unheard. Everyone works together to bring the best out in each other and the group. For this to happen, everyone must put their tribal differences aside and work together as one. Individuals must also be clear about their roles, which should be based on strengths. As a community, great things can happen when each individual contributes, according to their strengths, toward a common goal.

The power to fix the problems of Africa lies in the community. Communities can develop powerful solutions to eliminate the problems of Africa for good. We must learn to leverage the power of the community to make an impact. Everything does not have to be done on a large scale or all at once. **Small steps in the right direction, with regular interactions among the people who are collectively committed to a common purpose, can begin the process of change and growth.** Let us all work together toward a better Africa.

CHAPTER 23: TRUST AND BELIEVE THAT YOU HAVE WHAT IT TAKES

Never give up on yourself, because you have what it takes.

Nothing is off-limits for you when you believe you have what it takes. The knowledge of this is the foundation on which a lot of success is built. Unfortunately, many people struggle in this area. To achieve your goals, you must first believe in yourself and your abilities. A lot of people fail today, not because they don't have what it takes to be successful, but because they don't believe they have what it takes to achieve the success they desire. This makes it difficult for you to tap into your internal abilities. You are full of immense abilities and potential; all you have to do is uncover and apply it all. Believing in yourself and knowing you have what it takes is important for your success.

The belief should be so strong and firmly rooted that you can actually picture yourself living out your dream. We all have dreams and aspirations in life, but having a strong belief that you can achieve them plays a big part in whether or not those dreams become reality. Your belief systems shape the way you think and ultimately the actions you take. Program your belief system to work to your advantage by having a "can-do" attitude. When you come across a challenging situation, notice the difference when you face it with a "can-do" attitude as opposed to a "I'm not sure if I can do this" attitude. Say to yourself: "I can do this, I have what it takes." As you repeat this over and over again, you feel a change inside you; all of a sudden, the thing that looked challenging before no longer does. You feel different about yourself and you are more willing to take on the challenge. To get the desired results, your belief systems should always match what you are trying to achieve.

Many Africans feel powerless because they attribute certain problems to evil. But they are giving the evil power and authority over their lives. **There is no denying that there is evil in this world, but the light will always conquer the darkness.** By shining more light into your life, you can essentially drive off all darkness. Instead of attributing every bad thing that happens to evil, walk toward the light and drive all darkness out of your life. There are certain things in life that we bring upon ourselves that have nothing to do with evil. It is about us. Through idleness, laziness, lack of resourcefulness, and so on, we bring certain situations upon ourselves. Sometimes we just need to look within to find out what the problem is. We need to find out where we went wrong and discover how to fix the problem.

Too many times, people say they cannot do something, even before they attempt it. Conceding to defeat before undertaking a task is setting yourself up to fail. When you tell yourself that you cannot do something, your whole being acts like you cannot do it. When you start doing it and you fail at it, it is no surprise at all, since you already told yourself you could not do it. Again, do not concede to failure; you have what it takes to get it done.

You will come across situations in life that you do not feel prepared to handle. In those situations, you might have to learn something new or acquire a new skill. Know that there is nothing you cannot learn; there is no skill you cannot master, but if you concede to failure, then you will not get it done. Everyone has at one time started as a novice. By applying themselves and staying committed to their goal, they were able to master it. You are no different. If you are not a master at it yet, it only means you are in the same situation as those individuals when they first started. You need time to develop yourself; with time, you too will become a master at it.

A lot of people examine their lives and believe they cannot make a difference, believing they do not have what it takes to make a difference for themselves or for the people around them. They try to justify this feeling of inadequacy by making various claims. But all these claims they make are nothing but excuses. Some people claim they have no freedom. To those people, I say examine the life of Nelson Mandela and see what he was able to accomplish. Some people also say that they have lost too many years of their lives due to the actions of others. To those people, I say take another look at the life of Nelson Mandela and see what he was able to achieve, even after twenty-seven years in prison. Some people also claim that they cannot do anything to contribute toward equality and the civil rights of the people around them. To those people, I say examine the life of Martin Luther King, Jr. Some people claim they do not have the necessary tools to develop their ideas and that it's impossible to build the things they dream of. To those people, I say examine the great pyramids of Egypt. Even with today's tools and technology, it would take a lot of effort to recreate the pyramids. There are no excuses. You have what it takes.

It is perfectly okay to dream and think big for yourself. Dreams are a way of using our imagination to our advantage. Your imagination and dreams have no bounds. With a good work ethic and a relentless drive, you can live out your dreams. Never be scared to dream; always remember that your dreams are achievable. Imagine if Martin Luther King, Jr. had been scared to dream. Imagine if he had thought that his dream was not possible. If he did, he would never have made the kind of impact he did. Dream big dreams, and when you wake up, take action toward those dreams, knowing fully that you have what it takes to make your dreams come true.

Another reason why people fail to pursue their dreams is insecurity. They feel they are not good enough to achieve their dreams and that they lack the ability to make their dreams come true. They are not sure of themselves or certain about what they are capable of doing. For these and other reasons, they doubt their dreams. If this is you, I need you to change how you feel about yourself. Get rid of all the false beliefs that you have of yourself, and instead develop some positive beliefs. You are more than a conqueror. You were made for this. You were made to triumph. You have what it takes in you and there is no reason for you to think less of yourself.

Believing that you have what it takes gives you confidence in yourself. The lack of self-confidence leads to performing dismally at things that you would have otherwise been good at. Self-confidence allows you to move toward achieving your goals and desires. Feed your mind with thoughts that empower you and that fill you with the needed belief and confidence to go after what it is you want. As you do this, you will build up your confidence till you get to the point where you are no longer scared to pursue your goals.

Believing that you have what it takes also gives you the encouragement you need to press on. When you feel like quitting, knowing that you have what it takes at the back of your mind gives you the energy and encouragement you need to keep going. Sometimes all we need is encouragement. You might have thought it was over. You might have thought you did not have a chance, but with the right encouragement, you can get back on your feet again. You can muster the willpower inside you to give it a shot again. This is why it is important to encourage others. When they are down and they too think it's all over, your words of encouragement could mean the difference between failure and success.

Trust yourself; don't let the feeling of inferiority stop you from doing what you need to do. Don't think you aren't good enough to do something or worthy enough to achieve a goal. Remember: You are not inferior to anyone. You are a human being, just like everyone. You are by no means a substandard person. You are more than good enough to achieve your goals. Placing a higher value on yourself is important for your success. As you achieve more and more success, it will help you feel better and better about yourself and your abilities. You cannot get to that point unless you give yourself a chance. Your success depends on it.

Trusting yourself and knowing that you have what it takes doesn't mean you can ignore the advice of others. Be open to receiving constructive feedback from others. If others give you advice that can help you, then, by all means, follow their advice. Everyone has room for improvement. Even those at the very top of their game can still improve. You, too, can always get better. You can always do better, so don't pass on an opportunity to improve yourself.

Have you ever had to choose between two choices, and something inside told you to go with the first choice, but you decided against it and went with the second choice, which ended up being the wrong choice? That something inside you is called your gut feeling or intuition. Sometimes you have to trust it and allow it to guide you. It is very common to hear stories of people who, after making a bad decision, will say, "Something told me not to do it" or "Something told me not to trust this person." That something they are referring to is their gut feeling. You have it inside you; it speaks to you and it is meant to guide you. It is there to equip you with what it takes to make the right decisions. This is similar to what the animals used in the story about the animal migration at the beginning of this book. The animals have to trust their gut feeling when they are wandering around and sense danger. Their gut feeling tells them when it is okay to stay and when they must run to avoid predators. You, too, have to get in touch with your gut feeling and learn how to properly apply it.

Success and greatness is not just in some of us; it is in all of us. We all have the ability to tap into the power that lies within. Sometimes all that is required is trusting ourselves, no matter what anyone else thinks or says. Believe in yourself and keep on working toward your goals with all that you have in you. Move forward with all your might and power. Apply yourself with all your abilities and trust that what you are doing will work out. Your belief and confidence will drive you to make it happen. You will run into bumps along the way. Everyone does. Trust and believe that you have it within you to find solutions to those bumps.

If anything, one of the things I would like you to take out of this is the message of hope. Hope that you can do anything that you set your mind to. Hope that your dreams can come true. Too many people have given up hope in the system and all that it was intended to do. They resort to illegal means to provide for their daily bread. If you are one of those people with a broken spirit who has given up all hope, I want you to know that it is not over. You are still in the race. You have the ability to finish the race, regardless of your situation or position, regardless of what people around you say. You can still do it. Take on a new challenge, pursue your dreams, go after your goals, and remember to trust and believe that you have what it takes.

CHAPTER 24: TRUST THE PROCESS

Different laws that affect our existence and how everything interacts with each other guide our universe. These laws, such as that of gravity, keep our feet on the ground when we walk, and mathematical laws make one plus one equal two (1+1=2). You can depend on the laws of the universe because they won't disappoint you. The sun will always rise and set every day. If you go anywhere on Earth and throw a stone in the air, it will come right back down, according to the law of gravity. Mathematical laws are also the same in every country you visit. One plus one equals two in Ghana, China, Mozambique, South Africa, Ecuador, Egypt, Nigeria, India, Ethiopia, Kenya, or any other country you go to. These laws are constant.

Of all the different laws, the law of sowing and reaping is one of my favorites. When a farmer plants his seeds, he trusts in nature and the law of sowing and reaping, which dictates that, provided all the conditions are met, he will have a harvest in due time based on what he planted. The farmer knows that the seeds will grow, provided that the plant gets the right amount of water and nutrients and the weather conditions are right. The farmer also knows that if he repeats this process in any given year, he will get similar results. This law is universal, which means that it is the same regardless of where you live. The law is also impartial, so it does not treat anyone differently. The law of sowing and reaping does not care about what family you are from, how old you are, whether you are rich, or whether you are poor. Anyone who applies these laws will get similar results if they go through a similar process.

You Have a Choice as to What You Sow and When You Sow

Whether you choose to sow or not to sow, the choice is ultimately up to you. If you choose to sow, you know you will eventually have a harvest; if you choose not to sow, you cannot expect to have a harvest. You can also choose which crop you sow and when you sow it. There is a good time to sow and a bad time to sow, but the choice of when you do it is completely up to you. A person who sows during the rainy season and a person who sows during the dry season will get different results. This is the same in life. We have a choice of when to take appropriate action. Whether you take action at a good time or at a bad time will affect the type of results you get. We also get to decide what type of action we take, with each action bringing about different results.

You Must Know About the Crop You Plant
Take the time to learn about the crop you are planting so you know what to expect from it. You have to know the best time in the year to plant your seeds, how much water it needs to grow, how long the growing season is, what it takes to maintain the crop, what type of pests to look out for, and so forth. You must know a lot about the crop so you can make good decisions throughout the season. The same thing happens in life. When you are trying something new, you must educate yourself to make good decisions. If you want to start a new business or career, you must learn about it so you know what to expect in the future. The information you gather will help guide you as to whether it is the right move for you to make or not.

You Reap According to What You Sow
What you plant determines what you harvest. If you plant tomatoes, then you can expect to reap tomatoes. If you plant oranges, then you can expect to reap oranges. If you plant bad seeds, you can expect a bad harvest. If you plant good seeds, you can expect a good harvest. The point of this is that what you plant and what you sow are directly related. You cannot plant tomatoes and expect to reap oranges at the end of the season. What we get back in life is a direct measure of what we put into it. If you practice doing something, you get better at doing it. If you study more, you get better grades. If you do not study more, your grades do not improve.

What You Sow Multiplies When It Is Time to Reap
When you plant a seed and it grows, you can reap more seeds from the plant than you sowed. The concept here is that one single seed planted develops into a mature plant that bears fruits in multiples. If you plant an orange seed and it becomes

an orange tree, each fruit from that tree holds multiple orange seeds. Each seed from each fruit can be replanted to get more orange trees. In life, you can also get similar results. It is possible to start a business with a small amount of money; over time, if the business becomes successful, you can get more money out of the business than you put into it in the form of profit. The money you get from the profit can then be used to start and grow other new businesses.

The Entire Growing Process Is Not Visible

When you plant a seed in the ground and the seed germinates underground, the growth is not visible to you initially. Even though the roots are forming and the growing process is ongoing, it looks like nothing is going on from where you're looking. It is not until the plant starts to appear above ground that it becomes evident that a plant is growing. The same thing happens in life. When you put effort into something, you do not always see an immediate impact or result. It might take a while to start noticing that your efforts are truly making a difference; the time it takes for each person varies. It could take six months, one year, or even two years before there are any visible signs of progress. You cannot quit on the process just because you do not see an immediate impact. Even though you cannot visibly see the results in what you are doing at the moment, your efforts are forming roots and growing. Just like the plant eventually shows growth above the soil, soon enough, the results will become visible enough for you to see.

Sowing Is Not Easy

Preparing the ground for planting can be tedious: You must clear the land of debris and any unwanted vegetation; you have to prepare the soil so it is full of nutrients that the plants will need. As the plants begin to grow, you have to constantly weed the beds so they don't compete with the plants for nutrients or block them from getting the sunlight they need. The same thing happens in life. When you are starting something afresh, it might take time to get things right. What you do might require a lot of labor and hard work to get things moving in the right direction. You might have to do a lot of research to understand what you are getting into. You might have to educate yourself so you are fully prepared. It might also require a lot of your time and attention to ensure that things are done correctly.

The Process Takes Time

When you sow, you cannot expect to harvest the next day. It takes time for the seed to develop, for the plant to fully mature, and for it then to bear fruit. The laws of nature go into effect with time. The same thing goes in life. You cannot always expect to get the results that you want immediately every time. For example, you cannot expect to start school one day and then graduate the next. One reason people are always eager to get results right away is so they can celebrate. There is something called delayed gratification. It is something that you must learn to work on. With delayed gratification, you must learn to work now and celebrate later. It takes time for things to fall in place. Patience and trust in the process are very important elements to practice here. Trust that everything will work according to plan. Be patient enough to wait, knowing fully that things sometimes take time to work out.

After Reaping, Sow From the Harvest Again

Once you are at the end of the season and able to reap a harvest, soon it will be time to plant new seeds. If you do not plant new seeds, there will be nothing to harvest the following season. It is important not to consume your entire harvest, but to save some for the next sowing season. If you eat all that you harvest and save nothing for the following growing season, then you will have nothing to plant. If you have nothing to plant, then you will have nothing to harvest at the end of the next season. This rule also applies in the business world: If you have a successful business that makes money, you must set aside some of the profits to reinvest back into the business so it can make you more money. If you only take from your business and never put anything back into it, soon there will not be enough money to sustain it, and you will be out of business. On the personal side of things, always save a portion of the money you make from your salary or wages. Keep some aside for your future use. Do not blow it all frivolously. You never know when you might need it or what you might need it for.

Your Soil Matters

Seeds sown on rocky ground or in clay won't develop as well as those sown in good soil. If you sow your seeds in bad soil, you can expect to have either a bad harvest or no harvest at all. If you sow your seeds in good soil, then your plants will develop well, leading to a good harvest. Fertile soil gives plants the nutrients they need to develop properly while bad soil does not. In life, the same applies. The results you can expect are based on the foundation that you build upon. If you build a business on a foundation of lies, deceit, corruption, and illegality, then you can expect that you will reap as you have sown and all these things will be brought to light. When it is, bad publicity, fines, and other legal ramifications, not to mention going out of business, will follow. A business built on good governance, truth, openness, and trust can expect to reap the rewards of being good. The business need not fear any of the ramifications that happen as a result of building a business on a bad foundation. Your mind is just like the soil in which you plant seeds in. If you keep your mind fertile, you can expect to reap accordingly in your life and in your body, just as you have sown in your mind.

The Roots Are Important

When something is wrong with the root of a plant, it slowly makes its way to the rest of the plant. Eventually, you will see symptoms of the problem in the leaves, the stem, the fruits, and the entire plant. When the roots don't get the right amount of water or nutrients it needs, the entire plant suffers. The roots must also go deep into the ground to keep the plant standing upright. If the roots are shallow, the plant will be blown over by the first strong wind that comes. The roots represent your foundation on which your entire being is built. Your foundation must be solid. If your foundation is shallow and does not go down deep enough, the first wind that blows, which represents the challenges, tests, and setbacks that you will face, will blow you over. It is also through your roots that you can feed yourself with the right amounts of knowledge, wisdom, and other things you need for your growth and development. How deep are your roots? Where do your roots get their nutrients from? Do your roots supply you with all the nutrients you need?

The Weather Will Change Along the Way

The weather changes with time, and throughout the year, you can experience different seasons. Some represent the time to sow and some represent the time to reap. Just as we have seasons for sowing and reaping, life also has seasons for sowing and reaping. Sometimes these seasons don't act in the way you expect and when you expect it to. Sometimes, there are droughts when you are supposed to have rain, and sometimes there is too much rain when you are supposed to have a drought. Sometimes there would be too little sunlight when there is supposed to be a lot of it, and sometimes there will be too much sunlight when it is supposed to be cloudy. The lesson here is that you must always be prepared to adjust to changes in life. Sometimes things do not go exactly how you planned or hoped. Learn how to manage the changes as they come. In life, there will be bumps along the way. You must be prepared for the good times and the bad times.

There Will Be Pests

Pests, such as rodents, birds, and other animals, often attack farmers' plants, which then don't develop as they should. Some pests may attack the plants underneath the ground where they cannot be seen. Some pests might attack the plants out in the open, while some might attack at night when the farmer has gone home. These pests also represent situations and people in life that attack others. These pests represent people who do not want others to get the success they deserve. They do different things to derail others so they don't get the results they were hoping for. Just like the pests feed off the plants they attack, these people also feed off destruction. It is where they get their satisfaction and happiness from. You must put up your defenses against these pests. You have to be on the alert at all times so you don't get attacked when you are not watching. Prepare yourself so you are ready to act when the time comes.

You can tell a lot about a tree just by looking at the fruits. In life, the results that you get can also tell a lot about you and what you put into the process. The more you understand the law of sowing and reaping, the more you understand how it affects different areas of your life. As you develop a better understanding, you get better at applying the law for maximum results in different areas of your life. Sow now and reap later. Prepare now and enjoy the results after. Applying this knowledge wisely will completely transform your life. You can experience all the happiness and joy you want in your life by planting the right seeds.

Your mind is just like the soil in which seeds can be sown. What your mind returns to you is based on what you plant into it. If you plant the seeds of success, then you will reap success. If you plant the seeds of failure in your mind, then you will reap failure. It gives back to you what you put into it. The words that you speak are also seeds. As you speak words, they develop roots and grow. What you reap from those words is directly related to the words that you sow or speak. That is why it's important to speak the right words that will blossom according to what you want to see.

Money is also a seed. When you apply it appropriately, you can use your seed money to reap more of the same. When you begin to view money and the other potential "seeds" that you have in your life differently, you begin to open yourself to new possibilities.

The world that we live in is governed by different laws. It is important to understand how these laws work to win the game of life. You must work on mastering the game. Everyone has what it takes inside to play, but not everyone has a full understanding of the game. Develop an understanding of how all the different laws and principles come into play. As you develop this understanding, you begin to master the game. Once you master the game, the next step is to apply your skills. These are the skills you have developed over time through constant practice. You will also need to apply the right amount of physical and mental strength along with your skills to get the results you want. When you put this all together, you get the recipe for success.

LESSON VI: HONOR

I would prefer even to fail with honor than win by cheating.
—Sophocles

There was a time in African history when honor meant everything. During this period, honor was the chief motivator behind how people lived their lives and it affected everything they did. Honor back then was the ultimate prize to which people aspired. But things have changed. Honor is no longer the ultimate prize; it now seems as though other things, such as money, have taken its place. People now go to great lengths in search of money, as they once did in search of honor. Money is important, and there is certainly a place for money, but it does not belong on the same level as honor. Honor lies on a higher level than money.

Anyone can obtain money, but it takes a certain type of person to obtain honor. A thief can steal money, but like the age-old saying goes, "There is no honor among thieves." If you always think in terms of honor and make decisions with honor at the back of your mind, it will not only shape your character, but it will also keep you from getting into trouble. With honor at the back at your mind, there are some things that you will do and not do. With money as the driving force in your life, however, it is possible to make mistakes that will put you in trouble.

There will be times in your life that you will be challenged to choose between honor and something else. I am asking that you not sacrifice your honor for the sake of acquiring easy things. You might be tempted to cheat on an exam instead of getting the grade you deserve; I advise you not to cheat. You might be tempted to lie to get out of something instead of speaking the truth; I advise you to speak the truth. You might be tempted to steal so you can get something you desire; I advise you not steal. Put your honor before these things. When you do, you will be a better person for it.

A lot of the things you will come across will promise you quick rewards, but what you will later find out is that a lot of those rewards are temporary. In the long run, you will have to face the consequences for those quick rewards. Too many times, we hear of athletes who use performance-enhancing drugs in some of the biggest sporting events, like the Olympics, only to be stripped of their medals and accolades years later when they are discovered. In the short term, they have the medal in their hand and think they have gotten away with it, but things change for them when they get caught. They often have to face public humiliation and shame for their actions for the rest of their lives. If you ask any of them, they will tell you that if they could do it all over again, they would not have used the performance-enhancing drugs.

It is extremely important that you uphold your honor at all times, even when it seems tough to do so. A lot of people out there feel like they have to perform dishonorable acts while on the job just so they can keep their position. Do not be afraid to do what is right because of your job, status, or your position in society. **Your job, your status, and your position in society were not designed to stop you from doing the right thing, but to encourage you to do the right thing.** Remembering this simple truth will help you make the right decisions. Don't let anything stand in your way of upholding your honor and doing what is right. Even when your decision is unpopular, be steadfast in doing the right thing.

As a society, we should also learn to give honor where it is due. Whenever a public official is found to have done something dishonorable, the news always makes the headlines and everyone wants to crucify that official. I think it is time that people put in the same or a higher amount of energy and emotion into honoring people who do honorable deeds; they shouldn't spend it only on attacking people who are not honorable. The people who do these honorable deeds ought to be celebrated and rewarded for what they do to show appreciation for what they have done in a manner befitting their accomplishments.

If you are the type of person who walks and lives with honor but you feel like you are not getting the recognition you deserve, don't be discouraged. Keep on doing what is right; in due time, people will bestow honor upon you. **If you are a person of high integrity and you continue to carry yourself with dignity and self-respect, people will take notice and bestow honor upon you.** Even if you never get publicly honored, the greatest honor lies within you. It lies in the knowledge that you are living life with honor and displaying some of the highest human values that exist.

CHAPTER 25: HONOR YOUR PURPOSE

Have you ever wondered why you exist or what your purpose on Earth is? If you have, you are not alone. Most people think of it, too. I believe everyone has a purpose for their life. You are not an accident. You were put on this Earth to be something and do something. **If you have ever felt worthless, if you have ever felt like your life didn't count for anything, I want you to know that it does.** Your life is of great significance to not only yourself, but also to others around you. You are here for a purpose and everything you need to achieve that purpose is available to you. What you have to do is to first identify what your purpose is and upon identifying your purpose, honor your purpose by living it out. There are many steps along the way, but finding and living out your purpose is the goal. When you find out what your purpose is, you will know you have found it because of the deep connection you will have to it.

Most people go through life without ever discovering what their purpose is. They roam around life aimlessly, looking for its meaning. They are constantly frustrated and confused, and unable to get clarity on what their next step should be. There is a big part of us that searches for the meaning of life. A big part of us also wonders what our significance in life is. Finding your purpose gives life meaning and great significance. It helps your existence here on Earth make sense. No matter how bad things have previously been for you, discovering your purpose will make you feel more happy and alive. You will wake up every day full of excitement and energy and ready to tackle anything the new day might bring.

Finding your purpose helps you live your life with intention. By finding your purpose, you will wake up every day knowing where you are supposed to be and where you are heading. It allows you to go through each day with a set of clear objectives in mind as to what you should be doing and why you are doing it. Knowing what your purpose is alone isn't good enough until you take action toward it. By doing so, you can fill the void that most people have of not knowing what to do with their lives or what their lives stand for.

I believe each person has two kinds of purpose. The first is a purpose for you, your personal purpose. It's about your life and what you want out of it. Your personal purpose represents your highest personal goals and the highest version of yourself. It involves living your life to the very best of your abilities and leaving no ability undeveloped. This means that you develop yourself in every way possible. Your personal purpose also involves living life according to your highest values, discovering those that represent the very best of you and living your life according to those values.

The second kind of purpose is your higher purpose, something greater than you. It's something of great meaning and significance that is above and beyond just your own life. It represents something greater than just your personal goals. The impact of fulfilling your higher purpose is far-reaching and a lot of people's lives are touched as a result of you fulfilling your higher purpose.

Finding Your Purpose

Discovering and living out your purpose is one of the most fulfilling and rewarding things there is in life. If you happen to discover your purpose early, the beauty of it is that you have the rest of your life to live it out. The big question most people ask is, "How do I discover my purpose?" For those who do not know what their purpose is, I will attempt to guide you to find it. All throughout your life, you have received clues as to what your purpose is, but you probably never paid close attention to those clues. To discover what your purpose is, there are a few things that you can do to discover it.

Discovering your purpose starts with asking the right questions. Go somewhere quiet where you will not be disturbed. Once there, go into deep thought and ask yourself: "What is my purpose in life? What am I naturally wired to do?" Repeat those questions over and over again, pausing each time to think through the question. As you think through, dig deep into yourself and listen to your subconscious mind, or inner voice, for an answer. If you do this successfully, you should get a very powerful and inspirational answer of what your purpose is. Finding out what your purpose is will be so touching that it will make you want to cry. Some people actually do cry when they discover it because the revelation moves them deeply.

When you discover your purpose, it feels right and makes complete sense to you. Your purpose makes things clearer for you and gives you a deeper understanding of why certain things in your life have happened the way they have. You will feel energized by your purpose and want to take immediate action toward it. If you successfully discovered your purpose, I want to congratulate you. Just so you are aware, the energizing feeling that you are experiencing is completely normal. I also want you to know that your life from this point will never be the same again. Your life is going to change for the better. If you did not find out your purpose, repeat the exercise again over the next few days. Examine your life and think deeply about why you do the things you do. Be encouraged; your purpose will come to you eventually.

Another beneficial exercise is writing down the gifts, talents, and skills that you have. In addition to that, write down a list of the things you are passionate about and things that get you excited. Write down the gifts, talents, and skills that you know you have, even if you have only used them sparingly in the past. They could be things that you discovered that you did earlier in life but you never explored them further. Think thoroughly about all of these things and make sure that your list is complete. After creating this list, read through it carefully and ask yourself each time: "Why do I have this skill, talent, or gift? Why am I passionate about this?" Listen to your inner voice for the answer, and in that answer, you will find your purpose. Before taking action toward your purpose however, there are a few things you will need to do first.

Defining Your Purpose

Once you have identified your purpose, clearly define it. Write out what both your personal purpose and higher purpose are on paper. Make sure they are worded exactly how you want them to be, in a way that is easy for you to understand. This also makes them easier to follow. It may take several tries and edits before you get them just right, but that's okay. Invest your time into writing and making the necessary changes until they sound just the way you want.

Once you have them written down clearly, start thinking about the impact you would like to make with your purpose. Set some goals for yourself around it. What would it mean for you to achieve those goals? What would accomplishing those goals feel like? What would the highest version of you do? You will feel a sense of self-worth as you think through these answers. Henceforth, you will need to develop yourself because the bigger your purpose, the more you have to develop yourself to uphold that purpose.

Carrying Out Your Purpose
So now that you have identified your purposes and clearly defined it, you now must decide whether or not you want to honor it. Once you say yes to your purpose and decide consciously to answer the call, you must act on it. It is time for you to do the very thing you were put on this Earth to do. Finding the energy to carry out your purpose will not be a problem. You will be so excited to work toward your purpose that you will go hours upon hours on end without getting tired. Others will wonder how you can put so much time into it, but deep down, you will know it comes easily to you because you are passionate about it. You will be filled with so much enthusiasm and passion that it will be easy for you to work tirelessly toward your purpose. You will not need to force it; it will just naturally come to you.

As you begin to work toward your purpose, it will become the focal point of your life. You will begin to build everything around it. Your purpose will become something you think of every day. The feelings that your purpose stirs inside you will be so strong that it will constantly pull you toward it. Eventually, you will become one with your purpose; it will become who you are. You will pursue your purpose with total dedication. Your purpose will shape your life, giving it meaning and direction.

I believe life clears a path for those who are fulfilling their purpose. Things feel a little easier for you and smoother. Opportunities to fulfill your purpose that you never noticed before will become visible. As you follow your purpose, don't be surprised when positive things begin to happen in your life quickly. Things will start to line up for you at just the right time and everything you need will appear.

As you pursue your purpose and take steps toward it, you will attract the resources and the connections you need. It will be nothing for people from all over to help you fulfill your purpose. They will come from places you do not expect; some will ask you how they can help you fulfill your purpose and others will show up with the resources you need to fulfill your purpose without you having to tell them what you need. Your excitement and passion toward your purpose will attract people to you. Don't be alarmed by this; let them know how they can help you.

Fulfilling your purpose is one of the most satisfying things that a person can ever do. Pursuing your purpose keeps you excited and full of life and also helps you avoid boredom. When you are working toward fulfilling your purpose, there is no such thing as being burned out, tired, or weary. There will always be energy to do what excites you and what you love.

It will bring a lot of joy to you and to the lives of those you touch. You will feel good about what you have been able to contribute. Be on the lookout for opportunities to carry out your purpose. If you find you are getting weary, check and make sure you are still working toward your purpose. When you lose your purpose, you will start to fizzle out, lose energy, and lose your motivation. Do not let fear or anything else hold you back from delivering and sharing your purpose. When you carry out your purpose, the world becomes a better place as a result of your doing so. Most importantly, by fulfilling your purpose, you will know that you completed the work with which you were entrusted, that you finished the race, and that you fought the good fight.

CHAPTER 26: GIVING BACK

The value of a man resides in what he gives and not in what he is capable of receiving.
—Albert Einstein

Wherever you are in life today or whatever you have achieved, if you examine your life carefully, you will find out that someone at some point directly or indirectly contributed to your success, either through a helping hand, life-changing advice, financial resources, or other forms of support. The act of giving back is one way this cycle continues. Since someone else poured into you, it is only right that you pour into someone else. Even if you can't identify the specific person who influenced your life, your decision to give can start a whole new cycle of giving.

Going back to the sowing and reaping metaphor, every time you give, you are sowing. And you will reap according to what you sow. Every time you give, you are essentially sowing a seed, and whatever you sow as a seed will eventually take root and bear fruit. This means that when you give, you will receive in equal measure or greater value than you gave. When you give, it may not come back in the same form as you gave, but it comes back to you somehow. That is why some of the wealthiest people in the world are also some of the biggest givers. This is partly because they understand the power of giving. And despite all that they give away, they don't run out of money. In many cases, they end up having much more than they did before they gave. When you are generous in your giving, you will receive generously.

When you give, you set a cycle of giving and receiving in motion. The expectation of receiving, however, should not be the sole reason for your giving. But be sincere in your giving. Avoid giving out of pretense or giving reluctantly as much as you can. Give out of the goodness of your heart. When you give, you should give because you are being a blessing to someone else. Give because you understand that it may allow people to seize an opportunity they may not have been able to seize otherwise. With your help, however, they can now take advantage of the opportunity. Your giving could also open up new doors for people that could put them in a position to help others.

Having the ability and urge to give is something to be proud of. Numerous people out there have condemned themselves to be nothing but receivers. They go around looking for what they can get from others without offering anything in return. They are people who either refuse to give in any way or believe they have nothing to give. And there are others still who know they have things they can give away but have convinced themselves that they cannot afford to do so. They have talked themselves into believing that their whole life will crumble if they gave those things away. This way of thinking is incorrect; everyone has something to give.

These people do have things they could give away. But they may not feel comfortable or even know that they are capable. Nevertheless, they have the ability to do so if they really wanted to. The most important thing is having the desire to give. When you have the desire to give, you will always find a way to do it. A person with no desire to give will always come up with excuses not to: "The timing isn't right," "I will give tomorrow," or "I'll give when there is more to give." The person's excuse or reason for not giving may change, but their lack of desire to give remains the same. This is what needs to be worked on first. Until that lack is fixed, the excuses will only continue.

When most people think of giving, they automatically think of money. This is understandable, since money is one of the most popular things that anyone could give. When you look a little closer, however, you will realize that money is not the only thing you can give back. There are other things that are valuable to give, and each one is capable of making a difference and doing a lot of good. Not having money to give is not an excuse for not giving at all. There is always something else you can give back.

One of these things is your time. You could volunteer your time toward doing work that will benefit your community. You could also volunteer your time to a charitable organization that serves others. Sometimes just making available time for someone in need can go a long way. For example, showing support for someone who has just gone through a tragedy can help alleviate the pain they feel. Giving your time to help others is an extremely rewarding experience for both the giver and the receiver.

Give through the use of your voice toward a cause that is important to you. This could be toward women empowerment, education, equality, and so on. The greatest results come when you give your voice toward a cause you are passionate about, one that is personally meaningful.

Another way to give is using your voice to speak for those who cannot speak for themselves, for example, those who are oppressed or too afraid to speak out of fear of the powers that be. Use your voice as a show of support for someone else. This could be a situation where someone is voicing their view on something and just needs a show of public support to get their voice heard. You can also give your voice toward making a change in your community. You can also use your voice to raise publicity for something that people wouldn't otherwise hear about.

You can also give back in terms of the relationships and connections that you have. If, for example, you know someone who needs something and you also know someone else who has what that person needs, you can connect both people together through your relationships with them. This is a great way to give. By establishing connections between people, you are putting your relationships to work for the good of others. Look for opportunities to give back in terms of your relationships and connections; they are all around you, and through such opportunities you can help facilitate introductions between people. The introductions you facilitate could be the beginning of a new and lasting relationship.

You can give back through your talents, gifts, and skills. If you have a special talent that can be used for the good of others, explore it. If, for example, you are a talented singer or actor, you can entertain and bring joy to others. You can use your talents, gifts, and skills to bring hope to those who have no hope. You can use it to put a smile on sad faces. Additionally, you can also use your influence, popularity, and public image as a way to give back to those in need.

Another medium with which you can give back is through the use of knowledge and wisdom. If there is a certain subject matter you are knowledgeable about, you can share your knowledge with others. Sharing your knowledge with people who would benefit from the application of such knowledge makes everyone's life collectively better. There are many teachers and professors out there who exemplify what it means to share their knowledge primarily for the good of others. Most people would argue that it is their job to do so, since they get paid. But a great deal of teachers are motivated to teach, not because of money, but because they genuinely want to help people.

These teachers are driven by the passion to work for the good of their students, despite the fact that they could be making a lot more money in a different profession. They take on the teaching profession because they want to impart knowledge to their students, not because of the amount of money that they will make. Some teachers also want to improve the level of education in their community. They want to help create an environment where students can learn better and be better contributors to their society.

There are also people who use their knowledge and wisdom to make new discoveries and invent new things. For them, this is their way of giving back. Throughout the beginning of time, mankind has benefited from such discoveries and inventions. Discoveries such as antibiotics, electricity, gravity, and the solar system have all shaped life as we know it today. Inventions such as the telephone, wheel, light bulb, airplane, and the Internet have also made life easier and more convenient. These discoveries and inventions are so important that it would be almost impossible to imagine life without them today. They have made us safer, live longer, be more efficient, and communicate better. The people who invented and discovered these things have given a lot to the world in value and benefits through their discoveries and inventions.

If you choose to give money, giving back financially can help you break dependency on money. Too many people today base all their dependence on money. For this reason, they hoard all the money they get for themselves alone without ever giving away any to others. If you believe in hoarding money for your use alone, learn to give some of it away. It can help you break away from your insecurities and your dependability on money. Even in religious circles, it is recommended that you give the top portion of your money away. This act of giving has been around for a long time, known as tithing. By giving it away, it is believed that it comes back to you more abundantly. You could also give away to charities in the form of donations to help support their mission.

It is possible that you might consider some of the different things and ways that you give as too small or too simple. But in reality, it is making a big difference to others' lives. Through your actions, you can touch someone's life in their greatest moment of need, where the impact of what you give is multiplied several-fold. As you have probably heard before, nothing is too small to give. Everything adds up. The timing of what you give could be such that it saves that person from falling into a situation that they may find unbearable and unable to get out of.

Giving back is a great way to connect to your community, to get involved with what is going on, and to show that you care about the people in your community. Giving back helps you develop a greater sense of responsibility to those around you. By giving to them, you show that you're available to help when needed. The decision to give back is your choice alone. Generosity is not something that can be forced; you have to want to do it.

As illustrated above, there are many different ways that you can give back if you choose to do so. Giving back is not really about what you would get from anyone, be it money, praise, or glory. Giving back should be about the person to whom you are giving. The biggest satisfaction comes from knowing that you have made a significant change in someone else's life. Giving also helps you develop a better feeling about yourself and the work that you are doing. Through your giving, people see the benefits of giving and its impact. Through your giving, you can inspire others to give. When others see you give, they know that they can do the same.

CHAPTER 27: LEAVING A LEGACY

When you no longer walk the face of this Earth, what will your legacy be? How will you be remembered? What will people say about you when you are gone? What will people think of when your name is mentioned? These are serious questions that everyone should ask themselves. They will make you think about your journey through life thus far and what all of it means. We are all at different stages in our journeys, but no matter where you are, ask yourself these questions. The answers will add value to your life.

Everyone leaves a legacy behind, whether or not they are aware of it. Some legacies are good, some are bad, and some are indifferent. When it comes to leaving a legacy, think of it in terms of walking with bare feet on the beach. As you take each step, you leave a trail of footprints behind you, and these are just like memories you leave behind for those who know you. These memories are what make up your legacy and what you will be remembered by. Through your legacy, people will know who you were, what you were about, what you accomplished, and what you lived for.

When working with wealthy individuals as I have done throughout my career, there is a wealth transfer tool we use called a dynasty trust. It is used to pass down a great deal of wealth from generation to generation. A properly structured dynasty trust could continue for hundreds and hundreds of years after its initial setup date. It is usually created by an individual who puts in a lot of money, which is usually in the millions, or property that will appreciate in value over time for the benefit of many generations to come. Through the use of this financial planning technique, an individual puts away enough money to take care of his or her children, grandchildren, great-grandchildren, great-great-grandchildren, and other descendants.

How much money do you think you will need to set aside to last your descendants 200 years from now? Is it $10 million? $20 million? Whatever that number is, it would take a pretty significant amount of money to do so because 200 years is a very long time. Despite this fact, wealthy individuals can still do it and leave a legacy. It is a way for them to be remembered and also a way to help their descendants financially. **While everyone cannot set aside enough money for generations to come, there is one thing, however, you can pass on, even if you have no money: a good name.** Honor will give you a good name and your descendants, generations upon generations from now, will benefit from it.

Leaving a good name is something that everyone can do. Unlike the financial tool above that is reserved for the very wealthy, a good name can be obtained by anyone. It isn't restricted to just the wealthy and doesn't require you putting away millions for years and years to come. It gives me great joy to know that it is accessible to everyone, irrespective of where you were born, where your family is from, or what you look like. A good name is a legacy that will last for generations. It will even outlast money and can reach heights that money cannot reach. There are various benefits to having a good name and we will take a look at a few of them so you can understand its power.

People with good names are celebrated. One of the most famous examples of a good name is that of Nelson Mandela. He is someone who was celebrated in life and in death. His good name will continue to be celebrated for years and years to come. Granted that Nelson Mandela is a global icon, there are lots of other people who have good names, but are not as famous. I am sure that you know someone in your community who has a good name and is well celebrated in your community. Even though the person is not as famous as Nelson Mandela, his or her contribution is still of great value.

A good name creates favorable circumstances in your life. It goes before you and makes your way easier. A good name also brings favor, not only for you, but also for everyone associated with your name, like family members, children, grandchildren, and other descendants. People will attach good memories and thoughts to your name. They will do things for those associated with you just because of their name and your legacy.

A good name will open doors for you that are ordinary closed. It will bring you opportunities you did not know existed because when you have a good name, people will seek you out to provide you with opportunities. They will insist that you know about an opportunity and all the benefits that come with it. That is how powerful a good name can be.

A good name earns you respect. A person with a good name is also well valued by others. This is critical because when you are well valued, people listen to you carefully and value your opinions more. Then you can push through with your ideas and get your point across, further increasing your level of influence. This is a major advantage and can be used to achieve even far greater deeds. But don't abuse this influence; use it wisely and in service to humanity.

A good name helps you make good judgment. When you have a good name, there are certain things you will and will not do because you have a good name to protect. This helps you stay away from doing dishonorable things that could potentially spoil your name. A good name helps you make good decisions by evaluating things thoroughly before taking action. A person with a good name avoids being dishonest, partaking in fraudulent activities, cheating others, and doing other things that could throw dirt on his or her name.

A lot of people who feel that they have bad names often believe that they have no name to protect. They believe they can do anything they want and they are therefore less likely to think through their decisions before taking action. Acting this way will most certainly lead to more trouble. Most people with bad names act this way because they believe there is no way back. A person with a bad name needs to understand that they are not necessarily stuck with a bad name. They can turn things around. It might take time to fix, but it can certainly be done.

You might have done things in the past that make you feel stuck with a bad name and that you are not worthy of having a good name. But regardless of your past, you can still turn things around. You have it within you to change what you think is a bad name to a good name. You just have to decide to change things for the better. As long as you are still alive, your story is not finished yet. You can still write your story the way you want it to be remembered.

To turn things around for yourself, use the same strategy that the person with a good name uses when making decisions. You can use these strategies to your own advantage. When contemplating a decision and you are not sure what to do, ask yourself: "What would a person with a good name do in this situation? How would the person act? What would I do if I had a good name to protect?" Your answers can go a long way in helping you make good decisions; they will have you thinking differently and ultimately help shape your actions.

When it comes to the matter of having either a good name or a bad name, there is something incredibly powerful that you must know: the power of association. Through the power of association, a person with a good name can strengthen the good name that he or she has and a person with a bad name can continue on with a bad name. It is especially powerful because it can turn things around. Through it, a person with a bad name can begin to develop a good name and vice versa.

The power of association refers to the type of company that you keep. The kind of friends and the type of people you have around you have a big impact on your life. As you spend time with them, you will begin to absorb and accept the way they look at life. You will pick up their habits and their ways, and start to do things in the same way that they do. As this happens, you also begin to get the same type of results they get out of life, whether good or bad. If you are trying to keep or develop a good name and you find yourself hanging around people who aren't doing things that are consistent with what a person with a good name would do, walk away. You might ruin your good name by being around such people. Being around them opens you up to negative influences through the power of association. Find a new set of friends that are in line with the type of person you want to be, friends that empower you and help you uphold your honor, friends that will help you grow in the direction you want to grow.

You can earn a good name by being of good service to others. Every time you help someone in need, you are building a good name. Every time you are of good service to your community, you are building a good name. By so doing, you are building your reputation as a person who cares about others and who also cares about his or her community. Your community will always have room for people who are willing to serve. Find out ways that you can serve and also add value and service to the lives of those around you.

Legacies are built on deeds. Your legacy is also determined by the outcome or results that are based on your deeds. All your deeds make up your story and your story makes up your legacy. Pay attention to your deeds and your actions, since this is what your legacy is built on. A legacy that is to be remembered positively is built through a lifetime of deeds to the benefit of humanity. Examine your past deeds to see what kind of a story it creates for you. If it is not the type of legacy that you want, then take action toward the legacy you would like to have.

Most people start to think of what their legacy will be when they are much older. They look back and try to make sense of it all, thinking, "Did I do all that I could have done? Could I have done better instead of making the mistakes I made? Should I have taken a different approach to life?" As they think through these questions, they begin to wonder how they will be remembered. You can start to think of your legacy even when you are young. The great thing about starting at an early age is that as you do so, you can begin to mold your life according to the legacy you want to leave behind by taking actions consistent with your desired legacy.

The legacy you leave behind becomes an example for others to follow. People who look up to you and admire your legacy will often look at your life for direction. If they want to leave a legacy similar to yours, they will examine your life for clues on how to create such a legacy. The story of your life gives them a map that they can follow to achieve similar results. There is no limit to the type of legacy you can leave behind: a great work ethic, a legacy of excellence, or a legacy of honor. The choice is yours and you have the power within you to make it happen.

Your descendants down the road will benefit from the legacy that you leave behind. Every time you make the right decisions or take the right action, your descendants can reap the rewards of what you are doing. For every legacy you build for yourself, you are also doing so for your family. People often look at children in relation to the memory of the children's parents or other family members. If the parents leave a certain legacy behind, the children are often viewed with that legacy in mind. If the parents leave a legacy of a great work ethic, the children are often viewed as having a great work ethic. If the parents leave a legacy of excellence, the children are often viewed as being excellent. If the parents leave a legacy of honor, the children are often viewed as being honorable. It is now up to the children to prove to people whether they were wrong or right in the way that they are viewed.

At some point, everyone dies. Even though human lives have limits and eventually come to an end, your legacy does not. **Your legacy is that one thing that outlives you and continues beyond your death.** There are people who died hundreds of years ago, but who, through their deeds, left lasting legacies behind. They are still talked about today and will continue to be talked about for a very long time.
The type of legacy you leave behind and how you will be remembered matters. What will your legacy be? You can, at this very moment, start working toward what your legacy will be. Right now, you can begin to shape your legacy in the way that you want to be remembered. You are more than capable of doing so, regardless of where you currently are in life. Start your journey with a simple step in your desired direction and let your steps leave a lasting legacy.

CHAPTER 28: THE AFRICAN PRIDE

Your pride for your country should not come after your country becomes great; your country becomes great because of your pride in it.

If you look at the great countries of today, you will find that the people of those countries take a lot of pride in their country. They are patriotic in every way. They treat their national flag with respect, sing their national anthem, and talk about their country in an honorable way. This same level of pride filters down all the way to the children who are taught at an early age to be proud of what their country represents. At first glance, it's easy to misunderstand this. It's easy to think that they all have this sense of pride because their country is already great. But, really, their country is great because they first had pride in it. The fact that the country is now great only serves as proof and a reason for them to continue to be proud of it. Pride comes with belief and when you believe in something, you are passionate about it, you care more for it, you work harder on it, and you do things to a higher standard. That is what makes a country great, that is what makes a continent great, and that is what will make Africa as great as it should be.

Too many Africans have lost hope in their countries. If you feel this way, I want you to be encouraged. Don't lose hope in your country because of a politician or economic situation. Be proud of your country's history; be proud to be African. Be proud of who you are and where you are from. Don't let anybody take that away from you. Believe in the possibilities of Africa as a continent moving closer to fulfilling its potential. Politicians and the government are not greater than any country. The country is greater, and you along with everyone else represent the country. If you don't believe in your country, you do not believe in yourself and everyone else around you. It is time for you to believe again. It is time for you to restore your African pride.

An African who does not have pride in Africa or its possibilities is actually a part of the problem, not the solution. Most people lose their pride because they don't see the results they would like to see in their community. It's human nature that when we don't feel good about a particular thing, we get discouraged and are unlikely to put more into it. But also a part of human nature is that when we feel good about what we put into something and what we get out of it, we are more likely to put more into it because the result matches what we want to see and thereby increases our belief in it. As our belief grows, we feel compelled to put more into it.

When you don't put anything into something, nothing comes out on the other end. In the same way, the lack of pride and belief that prevents you from acting toward Africa's progress actually ends up hurting you. If all you do is complain about how bad the system is and how broken the economy is, but you don't do anything to help fix it, you cannot expect to get anything out of it. Instead of complaining, get busy working toward a solution. Do your part to address these problems; to get the desired results, it's going to take everyone's best efforts and belief in the possibilities of Africa. No contribution is too small and no effort will be wasted. Even when things move slowly, take pride in your work and the reason why you do it. You will help make Africa's possibilities become a reality for the greater good of all Africans.

The media's portrayal of Africa doesn't help matters much. So much is said about how foreign media outlets negatively portray Africa, but you cannot let this affect your African pride. Africans are regularly portrayed as a primitive, uneducated, hungry, and poor group of people. Africa is further depicted as a continent full of people living in the bushes and chasing wild animals all around. There is no doubt that these negative stereotypes are demeaning and disrespectful. Rather than letting this offend you, look at it as a challenge. Let your life prove the stereotypes wrong. Let your life serve as an example of what an African can achieve. **Live your life with such greatness that it becomes the view that people have of Africans. Let your life become the new African stereotype**. Live your life with African pride.

Many things need to improve in Africa, but there are also a lot of good things about it. To avoid any negative stereotypes or misleading information, Africans must educate the rest of the world on how they want to be viewed. It should not be left to anyone else to define who Africans are. As an African, when you meet a non-African, make an effort to tell this person about Africa from your viewpoint. Tell them how things really are so they know. Africa is not beneath any other continent; it is full of hardworking and hospitable people. We need to do a better job at showcasing the good in Africa so it is not solely viewed in a negative way.

You have a big part to play with how Africa is viewed and talked about. People will often treat what is yours as well as you treat it. If you live in a house that is always dirty, whenever you have a visitor at your house, they will treat your house in the same way you treat it. They will leave things lying around your house and will not clean up after themselves. They will walk around your house with filthy shoes and not worry about dirtying your floors. As far as they are concerned, the house is already dirty, and since you do not care about your house enough to clean it up, then they won't care about dirtying it up. The same thing goes with your pride in Africa. Restoring the African pride starts with you. If you talk about Africa with pride in an honorable way, people will follow your lead and treat it the same way. Don't badmouth where you are from; instead, speak about it with pride. If all you do is complain about how bad things are and how terrible it is, then the people you are talking to will do the same.

Whenever a country wins a sporting tournament like the Africa Cup of Nations, people usually take to the streets in large crowds to celebrate. They scream, they dance, and they celebrate the victory in any way they know how. I have seen people burn car tires, honk their car horns continuously, or just run up and down the street in celebration. People will wave their country's flag frivolously and sing their national anthem at the top of their voice, overwhelmed with joy. They are experiencing pride. They feel proud to be associated with their country and they are also proud of the sporting achievement of their country. At that very moment, they are pleased to share their joy with everyone. While celebrating, the national pride that each person in the crowd has for their nation is the type of pride I want to see in you.

I wish people would have this feeling more often, not just because they won a sporting event, but also because they are just proud to be African. I am not asking that people go out on the streets, burn car tires, or honk their car horns continuously, but rather I want them to feel the same amount of joy and pride on the inside about their country and continent. Everyone celebrates when such a thing happens. At that moment, it does not matter how they feel about the government, their community, or any problems that they have; they just go out and celebrate. Have that same devotion to the growth of your country. No matter how you feel about someone else or a particular situation, put in your best for your country. If a sporting event can bring everyone together and give them a reason to celebrate, there has to be something else that is good about that country to bring everyone together and give them a reason to be excited and proud.

Show your pride for your country by honoring its ideals and being true to what your country stands for. Another way is to obey the laws of the land and be an upstanding citizen. Your devotion to obeying the laws of your country says a lot about the type of person you are. Your demonstration of leadership by example will encourage others to do the same. Stay active in your nation's building process. **Do not solely identify yourself as a member of a particular tribe, group, or family; think of yourself as a member of one nation.** The combination of everyone's differences is Africa's strength. **Let us no longer use Africa's diversity as a tool to divide us, but instead, let it be a tool that brings everyone together.** By working together as one, everyone will be able to bring honor to Africa.

If your belief in Africa has been shaken or you don't have pride in Africa, remain encouraged; you can take steps to build up your pride. First, make a list of your favorite memories about Africa and the things you like most about it. Once the list is created, look at it often and draw encouragement from it. In addition to using the list to shore up your pride for Africa, read the words below about Africa and being African. Keep it with you and read it when you need encouragement and when you feel that your African pride is being tested.

Most people write me off when they see me.
They do not know my story.

WEALTH FOR ALL AFRICANS

They say I am just an African.
They judge me before they get to know me.
What they do not know is
The pride I have in the blood that runs through my veins;
The pride I have in my rich culture and the history of my people;
The pride I have in my strong family ties and the deep connection to my community;
The pride I have in the African music, African art, and African dance;
The pride I have in my name and the meaning behind it.
Just as my name has meaning, I too will live my life with meaning.
So you think I am nothing?
Don't worry about what I am now,
For what I will be, I am gradually becoming.
I will raise my head high wherever I go
Because of my African pride,
And nobody will take that away from me.

Like everywhere else in the world, Africa has a long list of problems. As much as some people like to act as if those problems don't exist, we must come to terms with the fact that it does and it is the only Africa we have. We cannot hide from these problems or choose to ignore them; we must tackle the problems Africa faces, and, together, we will prevail.

A common thing I used to hear when I was growing up in Africa was how things used to be really good back in the day. It is a common story that is often told to the younger generation. The story is about how good things used to be and how life was so much better. My guess is, at some point in your life, an older person probably told you something similar, along the lines of "In the olden days," "Many years ago," "A long, long time ago,"…things were really good in Africa.

So how did things get to be the way they are now? Did it happen overnight? No; it was a gradual process. For this reason, it makes sense that, for Africa to claim its greatness, it too will be a gradual process. The signs are there. The rebuilding efforts are on their way, but there is still work to be done. A lot of talking has occurred, but not enough action. It is now time to act.

Action is what makes the difference, and the power to act is in *you*. There is no time to waste. There is no time to wait for some hero to come and save you and everyone else. That hero is you. Yes, you. You are already here and you have a contribution to make. As you commit to doing your part in the building process, the scale will eventually tip and Africa will achieve its greatness. Now go on out there and make a difference. Through your actions and your African pride, you will bring honor to Africa.

Citation

Chapter 2

"mediocre." *Dictionary.com Unabridged*. Random House, Inc. 26 Jul. 2014.
 <Dictionary.com http://dictionary.reference.com/browse/mediocre>.

Tell us your success story

Was this book helpful to you in any way? We would love to hear the impact this book has on your life. You can also contact Idowu Koyenikan, the author of this book, through any of the channels below:

Website: www.IkElevates.com
E-mail: IkElevates@gmail.com
Twitter Handle: @IkElevates
Facebook Name: Ik Elevates